S0-CPE-448

# The ULTIMATE IQ CHALLENGE

Marcel Feenstra
Philip J. Carter
Christopher P. Harding

WARD LOCK

A WARD LOCK BOOK
First Published in the UK 1994
by Ward Lock
Villiers House
41/47 Strand
LONDON
WC2N 5JE

A Cassell Imprint

Copyright © Marcel Feenstra, Philip J. Carter and
Christopher P. Harding 1994

All rights reserved. No part of this publication may be reproduced in any
material form (including photocopying or storing it in any medium by
electronic means and whether or not transiently or incidentally to some
other use of this publication) without the written permission of the
copyright owner, except in accordance with the provisions of the
Copyright, Designs and Patents Act 1988 or under the terms of a
licence issued by the Copyright Licensing Agency, 90 Tottenham Court
Road, London W1P 9HE. Applications for the copyright owner's written
permission to reproduce any part of this publication should be
addressed to the publisher.

Distributed in the United States
by Sterling Publishing Co., Inc.
387 Park Avenue South, New York, NY 10016-8810

Distributed in Australia
by Capricorn Link (Australia) Pty Ltd
2/13 Carrington Road, Castle Hill, NSW 2154

A British Library Cataloguing in Publication Data block for this book
may be obtained from the British Library.

ISBN 0 7063 7232 8

Design and typesetting by Ben Cracknell

Illustrations by Ruth Rudd

Printed and bound in Great Britain by Cox & Wyman Ltd, Reading

# Contents

# About the Authors

Marcel Feenstra was born in Rotterdam in 1961. A Senior Research Fellow of I.S.P.E. (International Society for Philosophical Enquiry) and a member of Prometheus and the Mega Society, he first studied literature and linguistics at the University of Utrecht, then computer science, before starting his own computer consultancy, HiQ Systems, in 1987. He is currently a dual degree student at the Fletcher School, in Medford, Massachusetts and the Amos Tuck School in Hanover, New Hampshire.

Philip Carter was born in Huddersfield, West Yorkshire, in 1944, and he is an engineering estimator and lay magistrate. He is the author of several books, including the Take the IQ Challenge series, and is editor of the newsletter of the British Mensa Special Interest Group *Enigmasig*. He is a member of the Mensa and Intertel High-IQ societies.

Chris Harding was born in the UK in 1944 but now lives in Australia. He is a member of several High-IQ societies, including Mensa, Intertel, Mega and Omega. He was the founder of I.S.P.E. and is a member of the

International Test Commission, which polices IQ test standards throughout the world. He has been listed in the *Guinness Book of Records* under 'Highest IQ'. Among his awards are life membership of Intertel and Biography of the Year award from Historical Preservations of America.

## Acknowledgements

Thanks are due to every one of the High-IQ society members who submitted material for use in this book. We have been delighted with the response, which made our final choice very difficult. Thanks also to all the High-IQ societies that ran our notice appealing for material in their journals. Finally, our thanks to all our respective family members for their assistance with the project and words of encouragement.

# Introduction

It is with great pleasure that we present our second volume of original puzzles and tests from around the world compiled by members of High-IQ societies. We hope that as a result of this book many of the puzzles, which may have otherwise been lost to time or not even compiled, will become classics in their own right. Collectively they demonstrate a high level of creativity, which we are sure you will find entertaining, challenging, often amusing and always thought-provoking. We believe that once you put your mind to work and think laterally, on the look-out for the unexpected, you will start to come up with many of the correct solutions.

High-IQ societies are international organizations that do not have the usual restrictions of boundaries and culture. Members are recruited on one criterion only: that of achieving a score on a supervised IQ test that puts the applicant in the top 2 per cent or, in the case of some societies, the top 1 per cent or higher, of the population. High-IQ societies are perhaps best described as social clubs that encourage contact between members through meetings, dinners, lectures, conferences or correspondence. No one member, or group of members, has the right to express opinions on behalf of the society. Because they are recruited on just the one criterion, all members are of equal standing.

The largest and best known High-IQ society is Mensa, which accepts for membership anyone who has achieved a score within the top 2 per cent of the population on a supervised IQ test. *Mensa* is the Latin word for 'table', thus suggesting a round-table society. Other High-IQ societies – the American-based Intertel, for example – have a qualifying level within the top 1 per cent of the population, while some are even more selective. The Mega society, for example, has its threshold at the 99.9999th percentile and accepts only one person in 1,000,000.

The puzzles that follow are, as might be expected, of greatly varying degrees of difficulty. To enable you to monitor your performance throughout, we have allocated the following star rating system.

☆ Standard
☆☆ More challenging
☆☆☆ Difficult
☆☆☆☆ Very difficult
☆☆☆☆☆ Fiendishly difficult

Each puzzle has been cross-referenced with two numbers: a question number (Q) and an answer number (A). This has enabled us to mix up the answers section so that there is no risk of your seeing the answer before you tackle the next puzzle. We are also including a compilation of IQ tests with assessment ratings. Finally we have listed below some High-IQ societies with contact addresses.

Good luck, happy solving and have fun!

**British Mensa Ltd**
Mensa House
St John's Square
Wolverhampton WV2 4AH
UK

**Mensa International Ltd**
15 The Ivories
6 – 8 Northampton Street
London N1 2HY
UK

**Intertel**
PO Box 1083
Tulsa
OK 74101-1083
USA

**I.S.P.E.**
Harry L Callahan
PO Box 34304
Omaha
NE 68134
USA

**Mega Society**
Jeff Ward
13155 Wimberly Square #284
San Diego
CA 92128
USA

# PUZZLES

## ANAGRAM PUZZLE

AUDREY AUSTIN, AUSTRALIA

A small repertory company touring overseas, placed an advertisement in English in a small, foreign-language newspaper. Unfortunately the type became muddled, and the advertisement appeared thus:

ALBINO THEREAT
SERPENTS
THELMA NO GATES
ACHE THING – NET HARPS
(TON SEATER DYNAMO)
RATS: LARCHES INWARD
STARTLE: RIDING TURNIP
PROCURED: SINNED ADVISE
CREDITOR: MARGIN WANDERS
CRIPES FORM THERE HANDOUTS LIAR

Can you interpret the original message?

## TRANSPOSALS

MITZI CHRISTIANSEN KUEHL, USA

A transposal is a word whose letters can be re-arranged to make new words – the letters of the word NAME can be used to make the words MANE and AMEN, for instance. Find the transposals in the verses that follow. For example:

A diner from Kalamazoo
Fished pesky black xxxx from his stew.
Said the waiter, with cool,
'The better to drool.
Imparts quite a xxxx with it, too!'

Answer: gnat, tang

1. Dame !&&&!&!!, harsh and grand,
   Vents all her !!!! on the land.
   She ices hills and fields below,
   And bends &&&& branches with her snow.

2. One gets !!!!!!! making a scene,
   But it's not easy !!!!!!! a teen.
   Sons are wearing an !!!!!!!
   And parents are fearing
   That it's not even for Hallowe'en

3. There once was x !!!!!-loving QQQ
   Decided to hassle a rat.
   The rat ran amuck,
   QQQx!!!!!?? struck.
   ?? died of rat rabies. That's that!

4. I'd rather sit in my /////xxx
   With book and steaming hot tea kettle
   Than brave the blasts of chilly xxx
   That ///// has sent to test my mettle.

5.  There is a story (apocryphal, perhaps, but no less interesting) about the curmudgeonly response made by George Bernard Shaw to a formal invitation from a certain society matron. Her name has been forgotten, hence the pseudonym in the invitation, which read: 'Mr and Mrs Vanderfeller Rockebilt will be at home Sunday afternoon, March 29.' To which GBS replied: 'GBS also.'

> 'Twas not the hapless xxxxxxx
> That GBS objected to.
> 'Twas just the xxxxxxx of the note
> And all that social ballyhoo.

6.  There was a fishwife from @@@*xxx*@**@
    Who loved to swill her xxx.
    Whenever she'd start to celebrate
    The blather would begin.

> She'd taint her @@@@@ with vulgarity,
> But 'twas her only fault.
> You learned to take it with charity
> And with a grain of ****.

7.  Cold ***///// night of snow,
    Yule log /////@ still aglow;
    Closest +++ suffused with ale,
    Worthy of a *+*+*+@ tale.

8. Viewed through the UUUU )))) of my
    jaundiced eye,
    UU)U)U)) are making me eat humble pie.
    They mess up my copy
    And make me look sloppy.
    Who can believe I've a good alibi?

9. They xxxxxxxxx me to make no claim
    That could be misconstrued.
    But no, I played the bidding game
    With great ineptitude.

    So now they've xxxxxxxxx off to me
    This ugly statuette.
    An xxxxxxxxx, probably,
    I never will forget.

10. That °°xx°xx° of summer months,
    Romantic °°°° with her allure,
    Has come to xxxx with us again,
    Still green and slightly immature.

11. My uncle John was not to blame
    For being in that house.
    !!!!!!!! haunts are not his game
    And uncle's not a souse.

    The truth is that he slipped and fell
    And to his great chagrin,
    He simply rang the wrong !!!!!!!!.
    The lady took him in.

# SHORT LIST

LLOYD KING, UK

Find the next word in this list:
Embark, Cotton, Ochre, Calm, Small, Duvet, Frost?

Choose from: Dell, Flute, Globule, Orange, Plume

# PROVERB

PETER SCHMIES, GERMANY

Use all the 42 letters in this array once only and travel in a continuous line, horizontally or vertically, but not diagonally, to form a proverb.

| L | E | T | T | H | R | E |
|---|---|---|---|---|---|---|
| E | M | T | I | O | B | A |
| N | O | E | W | U | T | K |
| A | T | O | N | N | N | I |
| E | M | Y | C | A | G | E |
| K | A | O | U | S | G | G |

# KEYWORDS

BOB NEWMAN, UK

```
G–H–Y–J–X–C–D–Q–L–W
\/\/\/\/\/\/\/\/\/
S–T–A–N–E–R–I–O–V
\/\/\/\/\/\/\/
F–Z–K–U–B–P–M
```

This is the unfamiliar GHYJXC keyboard, which is unlikely ever to replace the QWERTY one. The lines indicate which letters are considered adjacent to one another. We define a 'keyword' as a word the letters of which are all contiguous. It is not necessary for consecutive letters to be adjacent, as long as the letters of the word as a whole are. Examples are Owl, Hazy, Knobkerrie and Misunderstanding. Hyphenated words are permitted.

Here are some clues for keywords. All are straightforward definitions, more or less. The number of letters in each solution is given in brackets. Each begins with a different letter of the alphabet, although they are not in alpha-betical order. Altogether, every letter of the alphabet appears in the solutions at least three times.

1. Ancient Ship (11)
2. Answer (9)
3. Ask (7)
4. Attach (6)
5. Below strength (12)
6. Bet (6)
7. Canoe (5)
8. Cushion (6)
9. Die (6)
10. Exaggerated (7)
11. Express gratitude (5)
12. Garish (5)
13. Harness-maker (7)
14. Herb (9)
15. Horror-struck (6)
16. Indian harem (6)
17. Loss (11)
18. Old bicycle (10)
19. Pirate ship (5)
20. Plagiarized (7)
21. Platforms (8)
22. Sedative (7)
23. Shrubby plant (9)
24. Sociable person (5)
25. Toad (10)
26. Tree (6)

# SYNONYM TEST

ADAM ALEXIS, UK

In this example the line of letters above the keywords RED and VILLAIN has been used to complete the words CRIMSON and CRIMINAL, which are synonyms of the words RED and VILLAIN respectively.

MINALSONM
RED          VILLAIN
CRIMSON   CRIMINAL

In some of the questions a phrase is used instead of a keyword. You have 25 minutes to complete the questions that follow.

*A performance rating is given with the answers.*

1. CIIICRRLEALI

   RULE
   P _ _ N _ _ P _ _

   RULER
   P _ _ N _ _ P _ _

2. TDEETL

   SINISTRAL
   _ _ F _

   ADROIT
   _ _ F _

3. GYDGÉNIOYGETOOÉ

   PROTECTED PERSON
   PR _ _ _ _ _

   GENIUS
   PR _ _ _ _ _

   OFFSPRING
   PR _ _ _ _ _

4. FFAAFDAE

   PAY
   _ _ _ R _ Y

   RIOT
   _ _ _ R _ Y

5. ECFFAEEC

   INFLUENCE
   _ _ F _ _ T

   RESULT
   _ _ F _ _ T

6. DUEDUALDUIL

   REFER INDIRECTLY
   _ _ L _ _ E

   ESCAPE
   _ L _ _ E

   DECEIVE
   _ _ L _ _ E

7. SORADROSDEABORS

| RELEASE | TAKE IN | HOLD ON THE SURFACE |
|---------|---------|---------------------|
| _____B  | _____B  | _____B              |

8. IIILLEILI

| CRIMINAL | EVOKE |
|----------|-------|
| ____C_T  | ___C_T |

9. NAAEEIN

| CORRUPTIBLE | EXCUSABLE |
|-------------|-----------|
| V___L       | V____L    |

10. CATEETACEEREREI

| DISAPPROVE | DIMINISH |
|------------|----------|
| D_P_____  | D_P_____ |

11. ENIMENPOMCCPOE

| PRAISE       | COMPLETE    |
|--------------|-------------|
| __M_L____T   | __M_L____T  |

12. HESANIHESPROSYNHESSTHSEPRO

| OPPOSITION   | FALSE LEG   |
|--------------|-------------|
| ____T___IS   | ____T___IS  |
| COMPOSITION  | CREDENCE    |
| ___T___IS    | ___T___IS   |

## MISSING LETTERS

LLOYD KING, UK

KIW is to RKRHE as WANIB is to ?
Choose from KESDT, RDEAC, BOTG, UCAN,
HTY, TFS

## A WORD QUIZ

KENT L. ALDERSHOF, USA

**What do these words have in common – apart from having four letters?**

| | | | |
|---|---|---|---|
| ABLE | IRES | LICK | RAGS |
| ACED | LAGS | LIES | RAIL |
| ACES | LAIR | LINT | RANK |
| AILS | LAKE | LIPS | RAYS |
| AINT | LAME | LOGS | REED |
| AIRS | LANK | LOUT | RILL |
| ARMS | LAPS | LOWS | RISK |
| EARS | LASH | LUFF | RITZ |
| EAST | LAWS | LUKE | ROCK |
| EATS | LAYS | OILS | RUMP |
| EELS | LEAS | OLIO | USED |
| EWER | LEER | OURS | USES |
| | LEES | OWLS | |

# MAGIC SQUARE

PAUL ACKERLEY, UK

A 5 x 5 magic word square is one in which the same five words read the same both across and down. The answer to each of the five clues is a five-letter word that, when placed in its appropriate position in the grid, will form a 5 x 5 word square.

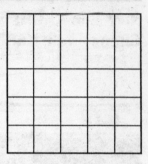

**Clues** (in no particular order)
Conspires
Insignificant
Banish
Tantalize
Concise

# SUM AND PRODUCT

PETER SCHMIES, GERMANY

A man goes into a shop, buys four articles and pays £7.11 for them. When he gets home he finds that if he multiplies the prices of the four articles with each other, the result is £7.11, too. What did each article cost?

# SUBSTITUTION

LLOYD KING, UK

If TA times I equals CAB, and TE times TILE equals CLOTH, what does TO times IN equal – BAT, HINT, POISON, TABLE or TOOL.

# FOUR-LETTER WORDS

MARCEL FEENSTRA, THE NETHERLANDS

Which word is the odd one out?

DENT      PIED
MAIN      REIN
NOSE      RIDE

# CANNY LASSES

RAY WILBUR, USA

What are the names of these young ladies?

1. Put her in a can and she becomes a North American.
2. Put her in a can and she becomes a warden.
3. Put her in a can and she becomes a boat.

# SCREEN SCRAMBLE

STEVE PLATER, UK

Here is a puzzle for the film buffs among you. Each sentence is an anagram of the title of a well-known film and of the name(s) of its star or (two) co-stars – the asterisks indicate the number of stars. There is a clue in each case to the film.

1. Farm moron shunned man if autistic (**)
2. Sinful reason why M ran to Rose – vice (*)
3. Hot jam in core – need fans handy (*)

# THE FENCE

MEL BEBEE, USA

A farmer has a triangular pasture that is 100 metres on each side. He wants to install an interior fence that will divide his pasture into two equal areas, but he finds the cost per metre of fence is very expensive. What is his most economical solution?

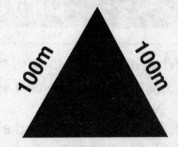

100m
100m
100m

# ALPHABET CROSSWORD 1

AUDREY AUSTIN, AUSTRALIA

Using all 26 letters of the alphabet, once each only, fill in the blanks to complete the crossword with good English words.

| A | B | C | D | E | F | G | H |
| I | J | K | L | M | N | O | P |
| Q | R | S | T | U | V | W | X |
|   |   | Y | Z |   |   |   |   |

# REBUSES

MITZI CHRISTIANSEN KUEHL, USA

A spate of bad weather rebuses
(5, 4, 4, 8, 5, 11)


'This ///// ⒲ makes the month replete,'
   Said Alice, mid a tea.
'Don't mind the ⒲, nor even heat;
   But hate ITHUY.'
'The time has come,' the ///// Hare said,
'To break this party up.
I spy a looming $\frac{HEAD}{TH}$
And hate rain in my cup.'

# SEQUENCES

CHRIS HARDING, AUSTRALIA

Insert the missing letters in the two lines
below.

Q ? T U O A D ? J L X V N

? R ? I P S F H ? Z C B ?

# CROSS DOMINOES

SUSAN THORPE, UK

We have an incomplete domino set. All those with halves of five spots or six spots are missing, so that the highest number is the double four. The set, up to and including the double four, is complete – 15 dominoes in all. Insert these 15 dominoes into the cross in such a way that the sum of the spots of the eight dominoes in the vertical row is 50 per cent greater than the sum of the spots of the seven dominoes in the horizontal row. Adjacent dominoes have, of course, to have equal numbers of spots.

**25**

# G-R-R-RIDDLE 1

MITZI CHRISTIANSEN KUEHL, USA

In the following crossword puzzle a letter or letters occupy the squares to form complete words horizontally and vertically. The number in each square represents the number of letters to be placed in that square – for example, there are three letters in square 1-1.

|   | 1 | 2 | 3 | 4 |
|---|---|---|---|---|
| **1** | ③ | ③ | ③ | ① |
| **2** | ① | ① | ① | ② |
| **3** | ① | ① | ① | ② |
| **4** | ① | ③ | ① | ① |

## Across
1. Decried; depreciated
2. Man-made watercourse
3. Archetypal milk dispenser
4. Greek letter (plural)

## Down
1. Olympic event; quoit
2. A model or pattern
3. Things to be done (as at a meeting)
4. Coin of Dutch West Indies (plural)

# THREE-CARD TRICK

JOHN CLARKE, UK

Jack King is the quiz-master at the Queen's Head pub quiz. Recently he asked a question that began with the words 'which three of the court cards in a standard pack...?' The three cards required were neither all of the same rank nor all of the same suit. Twelve teams were competing that night, and the answers submitted were as follows.

| TEAM NO. | ANSWER | TEAM NO. | ANSWER |
|---|---|---|---|
| 1 | Jack of Spades, Queen of Spades, King of Hearts | 7 | Queen of Hearts, Queen of Diamonds, King of Clubs |
| 2 | Jack of Diamonds, Queen of Clubs, King of Clubs | 8 | King of Spades, Jack of Hearts, Jack of Clubs |
| 3 | Jack of Spades, Queen of Diamonds, Queen of Clubs | 9 | King of Spades, Queen of Diamonds, King of Diamonds |
| 4 | Queen of Spades, King of Diamonds, King of Clubs | 10 | Jack of Spades, Queen of Hearts, Jack of Clubs |
| 5 | Queen of Spades, Jack of Hearts, Jack of Diamonds | 11 | King of Spades, Queen of Hearts, King of Hearts |
| 6 | Jack of Hearts, King of Hearts, Queen of Clubs | 12 | Jack of Diamonds, King of Diamonds, Jack of Clubs |

Jack was rather disappointed with the standard of these answers. Nine of the teams each named just one card correctly, while the other three (whose team numbers totalled 20) had none right at all.

What was the correct answer to the question? And what do you suppose the question itself was?

| Q22 | ☆☆☆ | A37 |
|---|---|---|

## SPOCKULAR

GEOFF HINCHLIFFE, UK

A hemispherical planetarium, 65 metres in diameter, contains a rectangular carpet, the four corners of which all just touch the outer wall. The image of Vulcan, projected on the ceiling, is a different integral number of metres from each of the four carpet-corners. If these distances total 180 metres, what are they?

# APARTMENT BLOCKS

LLOYD KING, UK

Which three windows in the last apartment block should be black?

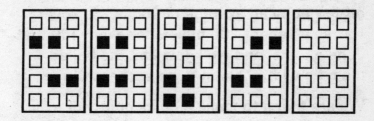

# DETECTIVE WORK

PETER SCHMIES, GERMANY

Five suspects – of whom one is guilty – have been interrogated by police. Who is the culprit, if just three of these statements are correct?

Al said: 'Don is the culprit.'
Bud said: 'I am not guilty.'
Charlie said: 'It was not Eddie.'
Don said: 'Al lies when he says that I did it.'
Eddie said: 'Bud tells the truth.'

## SHOOT-OUT

### CHRIS HARDING, AUSTRALIA

John and Harry are having a shoot-out because of Mary. John's bullets are off-target by an average of 30mm; Harry's bullets are off-target by an average of 60mm. However, Harry can shoot 200 bullets for every 100 that John shoots, and we know that the bullet must be within 20mm to be successful.

We are trying to make a quick quid, not a quick kill, so what odds are correct?

## BATH PUZZLE

### KEVIN N. STONE, UK

You have accidentally left the plug out of the bath and you are trying to fill it with both taps on.

Tap A takes 9 minutes to fill the bath.

Tap B takes 24 minutes to fill the bath.

The plug hole takes 36 minutes to empty a full bath.

How long will it be before the bath is full?

# LOGICAL JIGSAWS

### ADAM ALEXIS, UK

In each of the following, place the pieces into the grid in the correct positions in order to deduce the identity of the empty square.
For example:

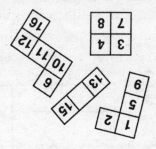

**Fit into the grid:**

| 1 | 2 | 3 | 4 |
|---|---|---|---|
| 5 | 6 | 7 | 8 |
| 9 | 10 | 11 | 12 |
| 13 |  | 15 | 16 |

It can be seen that the empty square should contain 14 to complete the grid in a logical way.

*You have 30 minutes to complete the six questions and a performance rating is given with the answers.*

**1.**

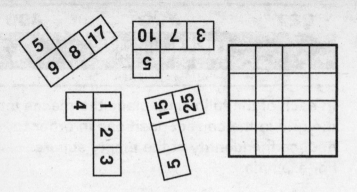

**2.**

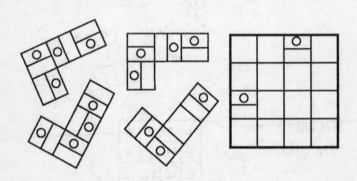

**3.**

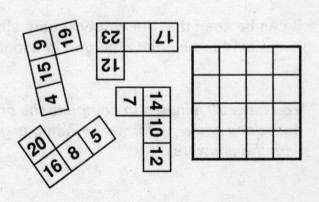

**4.**

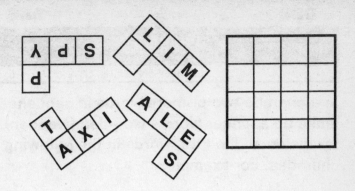

**5.**

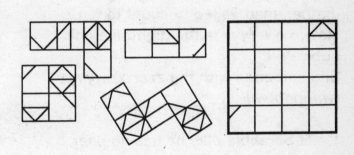

**6.**

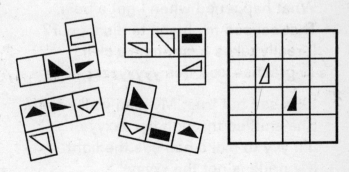

# CHARADES

MITZI CHRISTIANSEN KUEHL, USA

In a charade two or more words in sequence make up a longer word – woo-den (wooden), for instance. Find the words in the following charades. For example:

Xxxx, xxxx, Yyyy got the zzzz again.
Poor, Poor Will, whip
(Father, mad, failed to count to ten.)
Now, xxxx Yyyy in the nighttime chill
poor, Will
Sits and cries with the zzzzxxxxyyyy.
*whippoorwill*

1.  At Scrabble play he has no peer.
    I know I had a blank zzzz here.
    And he had zilch; he told me so.
    It's xxxx yyyyy now, I know.
    What happened when I got a beer,
    That caused my blank to disappear?
    It really takes a con-man's skill
    To practise xxxx this yyyyyzzzz

2.  ''Xxx sad but true: My man walked out,'
    She sniffled through her xxxyyy,
    'I'll yyy to make him see the light.
    My pride is not the xxyyy.'

# TOILETS OUT OF ORDER

JAMES HARBECK, CANADA

Motivated by the assertion 'there is nothing new under the sun', plus a dose of John Cage, Poetaster Escritor-zuelo, poet of little renown, decided to take quotes from five poems by a poet much better than he and re-arrange the words to make his own masterpiece. He even added two commas and a question mark!

You, of course, being intellectually voracious, are just dying to know who the poet is and what the poems and quotes are. Poetaster only let on that the sources are a love song, a prelude, something about a desolate place, one on empty humans and a Christmas piece. You have to work out the rest for yourself. The poet is the title of this poem.

The ancient unreal worlds
Gathering under the fog of death
Revolve with winter,
Fuel our ends.
Women go and visit.
Oh, what is it I should ask of the lots?
'Be but another way?'
Do not let us make a bang.
The world, like a vacant city,
A whimper in this brown dawn,
Is not glad.

# WHERE'S MY HOME?

KENT L. ALDERSHOF, USA

A lazy newspaper reporter wrote about a convention:

People gathered from many places. They came from Atro, Auda and Capa; from Feli, Fero and Rapa. More came from Saga, Sala and Tena; from Vera, Viva and Vora. Some came from Toni and Toxi; others from Scar and Velo.

Conventioneers were also observed from Dupli, Ethni, Lubri, Publi and Rusti. Many signed in from Loqua, Menda, Preda and Pugna. A few hailed from Preco.

Many other communities were also repre-sented. To name just a few, we saw badges from Compli, Infeli, Simpli, Pertina, Chromati and Perspica.

What word did he omit from his story?

# CRYPTIC WORD SQUARE 1

AUDREY AUSTIN, AUSTRALIA

A 6 x 6 magic word square is one in which the same six words read the same both across and down. The answer to each of the six clues is a six-letter word that, with the other five answers, will from a 6 x 6 word square.

|   | 1 | 2 | 3 | 4 | 5 | 6 |
|---|---|---|---|---|---|---|
| 1 |   |   |   |   |   |   |
| 2 |   |   |   |   |   |   |
| 3 |   |   |   |   |   |   |
| 4 |   |   |   |   |   |   |
| 5 |   |   |   |   |   |   |
| 6 |   |   |   |   |   |   |

## Clues

1. A century in foundation essentials.
2. Still burning a candle, perhaps?
3. Ringo's naughty Spaniard.
4. Disregard Ringo's mysterious trip to the East.
5. Century hero's odd jobs.
6. Snake rests uneasily, resulting in tension.

# ICEBREAKER

LLOYD KING, UK

Sherlock Holmes was relaxing in his study when a snowball struck one of the windows overlooking the street below, causing it to shatter. He went over to the window to investigate and, looking out, just caught sight of the Willoughby triplets, Danny, Mark and Oliver, disappearing rapidly round a street corner. The next morning he received this anonymous message:

> *? Willoughby. I am certain*
> *he broke your window.*

According to this, which one of the triplets should he question about the incident?

# KNIGHT'S MOVES

PETER SCHMIES, GERMANY

A chess knight makes two trips, visiting every letter-field once only and without leaving the respective square on each trip. What is the 15-letter word he spells in each square?

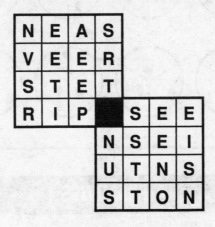

---

# RESERVES

KEVIN N. STONE, UK

In a game of 36 players that lasts for exactly 15 minutes, there are four reserves, who alternate equally with each player. This means that all players, including the reserves, are on the pitch for the same length of time. How long is that?

# SPOTS BEFORE YOUR EYES

LLOYD KING, UK

## What should go in the empty segments?

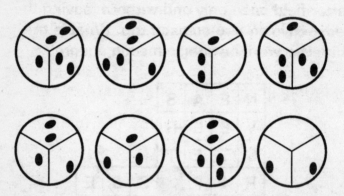

# ALPHAMETICS 1

MITZI CHRISTIANSEN KUEHL, USA

## Substitute numbers for letters in this addition:

```
  SHARP
+ SMART
───────
 MENSAN
```

There are two different pairs of closely related answers.

# AWESOME ANAGRAMS

SUSAN THORPE, UK

An anagram is an apposite re-arrangement of the letters of a word or phrase, e.g, FORGOTTEN is an anagram or ROTTEN FOG. Can you work out the following anagrams? The numbers in brackets indicate the number of letters in each word of the answer.

1. OH FEEL SHARP SPINES PET (5,5,10)

2. 'DECIS' MEET TONIGHT (3,3,6,4)

3. IN FAMED LIBRARY NOOKS (4,6,4,5)

4. OH MEND TENDER BREAK (2,6,6,3)

5. SEE THE COMPETITIONS (1,7,2,5,3)

6. TUT, A MISERABLE STORY (2,4,2,1,5,4)

7. OH ROGUE MAN-MENU (3,5,6)

8. THE 'MASTERMIND' CHAIR IS YOUR'S ROY (4,2,1,4,3,2,6,6)

# LETTER CHANGE

MITZI CHRISTIANSEN KUEHL, USA

In a letter change one single letter has been changed to make a new word – as in alter and after, for instance.

For example:
'You xxxxxx is getting worse again,'  *plaque*
The dentist said, severely.
'Avoid all sugar like the xxxyxx,  *plague*
And come to see me yearly'

1. A pessimist does not want cheer.
   He senses rain though skies are clear.
   ?????????? folk will always think
   +????????? horoscopes hoodwink.

2. 'She has yyyyyy her privilege,'
   The scandalized officials claimed.
   'We're not yzyyyy by stories that
   Her pics and she are being framed.'

3. There's xxxxxxxx at our house these days,
   We have to take some action.
   Fat Johnny is the cause of this;
   He can't reduce a xxzxxxxx.

4. The fallen queen held chin up high
   And no xxxxxx did she make.
   'twas after all a yxxxxx slip –
   The lapse in taste was their mistake.

5. A lady on a pedestal,
   Inspiring to behold.
   The xxxxxx of that xxxxxo now?
   One hundred-one years old.

6. When at night the wind is howling
   And Old Fido starts his growling,
   I am really almost xxxxxxx
   Someone's there behind the xyxxxxx.

---

**Q39**     ☆☆☆     **A85**

## THE UNRELIABLE CLOCK

KEVIN N. STONE, UK

I have a very unreliable clock. It was correct
at midnight, but began to lose 30 minutes
every hour. It now shows 4.00am, but it
stopped 5 hours ago. Can you tell me the
correct time now?

# MAGIC SQUARES

J. CANTARA, FRANCE

In each square fill in the remaining numbers between 1 and 25 to form two different 5 x 5 magic squares in which each horizontal, vertical and corner-to-corner line totals 65. Apart from the five numbers already placed, no further numbers may occupy the same position in the two squares.

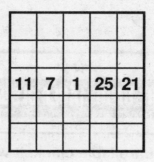

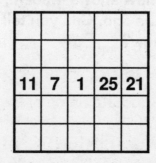

## QUOTATION

CHRIS HARDING, AUSTRALIA

Complete this famous quotation.

_ _ _   _ _ _   _ _ _ _   _ _ _ _   _ _  the

_ _ _ _ _ _   _ _ _  of  _ _ _   _ _ _ _  and all

_ _   _ _ _   _ _ _ _ _ _ _  some  _ _   _ _ _

_ _ _ _ , but  _ _ _   _ _ _ ' _   _ _ _ _   _ _ _

of  _ _ _   _ _ _ _ _ _ _   _ _ _  of  _ _ _   _ _ _ _

## ANAGRAMS

RAY WILBUR, USA

Can you solve the following anagrams? The numbers in the brackets indicate the numbers of letters in each word of the answer, and an asterisk indicates that a word begins with a capital letter.

1. A well-known title:
LEXICON FOR ADDING HISTORY (*6,*7,*10)

2. A well-known phrase:
TOOM AND THRAWN (3,5,1,4)

3. One word: 'MR POOCHY' IS (10)

4. And finally, find the name of a society of which I happen to be one of the original members: HAS GOT INTENTION TO BEAT AUSSIE COMRADES (*3,*6,*6,*9,*11)

# TRIPLE PLAY PUZZLES
### KENT L. ALDERSHOF, USA

These puzzles are solved by inserting the one-, two- or three-letter word fragments to make complete words. Each fragment is to be used only once.

## The Cat and the Rat

The one- and two-letter formations always fit either immediately before or immediately after the subwords shown within the puzzles.

1. CAT....... RAT.......
2. .CAT...... .RAT......
3. ..CAT..... ..RAT.....
4. ...CAT.... ...RAT....
5. ....CAT... ....RAT...
6. .....CAT.. .....RAT..
7. ......CAT. ......RAT.
8. .......CAT .......RAT

## Fragments

| | | | | |
|---|---|---|---|---|
| C | S | ADJ | GLY | PLU |
| E | S | ALS | HIN | REQ |
| E | DE | AVO | IDE | RIC |
| F | ED | BUR | LLY | TOC |
| H | ES | CAR | LON | UDI |
| I | HA | DEC | OBF | UIE |
| I | PA | DEH | ONA | UNG |
| I | RO | EAU | ONS | URE |
| O | US | EDR | OPS | |
| S | YD | FUL | ORS | |

# The Oriental Treasures

This is a double puzzle. First find the words by inserting the three.letter fragments, then read the third letter in each word to find a two.word description of a treasured item in a jewellery collection. (The ninth and tenth words are hyphenated).

1.  ...UMI......TION
2.  ...RCO......TION
3.  ...IST......TION
4.  ...LAS......TION
5.  ...LEC......TION
6.  ...TOC......TION
7.  ...NTE......TION
8.  ...PRO......TION
9.  ...-DES......TION
10. ...-PRO......TION
11. ...TRA......TION
12. ...DET......TION
13. ...QUA......TION

## Fragments

| | | | | |
|---|---|---|---|---|
| CHR | EGA | ICA | MIS | PHO |
| CIA | EGR | ICA | MPE | PRE |
| COL | ERA | INA | NON | PRO |
| CON | ERM | IND | NSA | REI |
| DEC | ETA | IZA | NUN | RPR |
| DEH | IAN | IZA | OMP | SIF |
| DIF | ICA | LIF | OSI | TIV |
| DIS | ICA | LIF | OVE | |

# THE SANCTIMONIOUS SERIES

KEVIN SCHWARTZ, USA

1. This is an easy, innocent, almost 'pious' series. Which digit comes next?
   2, 0, 3, 0, 4, 8, 1?

2. Which digit comes next? The puzzle may look odd, even if you circle around it.
   1, 1, 0, 1, 1, 1, 0, 0, 1, 1?

---

# ACROSTIC 2

MITZI CHRISTIANSEN KUEHL, USA

Solve the clues, transfer each letter to its appropriate position in the grid and a quotation will appear.

1. Flowering shrub   4 94 75 39 31 96 62 10

2. Musical accompaniment
   13 101 24 45 53 47 103 81 91

3. A native of Southwest Africa
   20 114 1 88 15 112 22 36 64

4. Related to Uncle Sam?
   57 106 12 41 79 14

5. Supplement, extension
   99 6 78 3 85 73 18 37

6. Boeotian   70 109 77 107 61

7. _____ Chorus   51 80 66 27 11

8. Fawning followers   98 65 69 9 84 72 90

9. Breed of dog
   28 104 2 71 110 83 102 16 108 25

10. Stealing   115 89 44 34 21

11. Wine:_____heimer   116 111 8 93

12. From C to chiming C   17 32 29 68 54 67

13. Where-ness   63 38 30 46 33 100

14. Igneous rock type   19 56 86 113 35 23

15. Asia Minor ancient   105 7 40 42 48 52 55

16. Bib and tuckered
    92 82 60 59 26 87 74 58

17. Battledore and _____ cock
    49 43 5 95 97 50 76

*Note: the first letters of the answers spell
out the author's name and the source of
the quotation.*

| 1 | 2 | 3 | | 4 | 5 | 6 | 7 | 8 | 9 | 10 | 11 | | 12 | 13 | 14 |
|---|---|---|---|---|---|---|---|---|---|----|----|---|----|----|----|
| 15 | 16 | | 17 | 18 | 19 | 20 | 21 | | 22 | 23 | | 24 | 25 | | 26 |
| 27 | 28 | 29 | 30 | 31 | 32 | 33 | | 34 | 35 | 36 | 37 | | 38 | 39 | 40 |
| 41 | | 42 | 43 | 44 | | 45 | 46 | 47 | 48 | 49 | 50 | 51 | 52 | 53 | 54 |
| 55 | | 56 | 57 | 58 | | 59 | 60 | 61 | 62 | 63 | 64 | 65 | 66 | 67 | |
| 68 | 69 | 70 | | 71 | 72 | 73 | 74 | 75 | 76 | 77 | 78 | 79 | 80 | 81 | |
| 82 | 83 | 84 | 85 | | 86 | 87 | 88 | 89 | | 90 | 91 | | 92 | 93 | 94 |
| 95 | | 96 | 97 | | 98 | 99 | 100 | | 101 | 102 | | 103 | | 104 | 105 |
| 106 | 107 | 108 | | 109 | 110 | 111 | 112 | | 113 | 114 | 115 | 116 | | | |

## A BIT OF A LARK

SUSAN THORPE, UK

Re-arrange the order of these birds so that they form a logical sequence.

DOVE  PEEWIT  BULLBAT  STARLING
PTARMIGAN  LARK  QUAIL

## GRANDAD'S AGE

KEVIN N. STONE, UK

My granddad was X years old in the year $X^2$. He is still alive in this year of 1994, old as he is! In what year was he born?

## SEQUENCE

PEARL CHIRPIT, UK

Which word will continue the sequence:

Dig, Minim, Militia, Sieve, Ave, ?

Choose from: Alibi, Avail, Oval, Valid, Mail

## THINK TWICE BEFORE YOU LEAP

MARCEL FEENSTRA, THE NETHERLANDS

What is the next number in this sequence?

17, 18, 19, 20, 22, 24, 26, 30, 31, 38 ?

## WORDS

JAMES SHELDON, UK

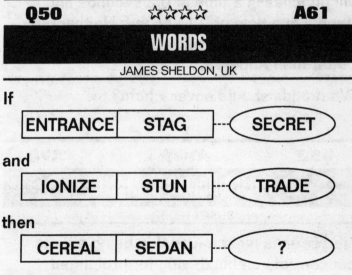

If

| ENTRANCE | STAG | ---- SECRET |

and

| IONIZE | STUN | ---- TRADE |

then

| CEREAL | SEDAN | ---- ? |

Choose from
1. Remote
2. Spy
3. Wheat
4. Ballet
5. Stage

# TRADING PUNCHES

CHRIS HARDING, AUSTRALIA

Two boxers are slugging it out. Jill U. is famous for her right cross and Angela Z. is famous for her upper cut. Jill has four other punches to her credit, but Angela has only two others. Each girl has a knock-out punch, but these are dispersed evenly between them. Jill punches in a time of 0.2 seconds and Angela in a time of 0.1 second. Neither girl has good defences, but Jill's are 50 per cent better than Angela's.

What odds should cover whom?

# PALINDROMIC ROMANCE

SUSAN THORPE, UK

Ned Eden is most unusual in being able to concentrate on his driving for prolonged periods of time without feeling drowsy, but he does drive slowly. Immediately before setting out on a long journey to see his sweetheart, Moll Lom, he noticed that the car's mileage was a numeric palindrome. Having made this observation and being of a precise turn of mind, Ned proceeded to drive the middle third of his journey, by distance, at exactly one and a half times the speed of the other two thirds. At the end of his travels he noticed that the mileage was again a palindromic one and, further, that the digit sum of the start and finish reading was 15 in each case.

If the romantic reunion between Ned and Moll took place exactly 24 hours after Ned set out, what were the mileage readings at the start and finish of Ned's journey?

---

**Q53**　　　☆☆　　　**A83**

# INSERTIONS

PETER SCHMIES, GERMANY

---

Within each group, insert the same three-letter word into each word to create new words. Note that the three-letter words are to be inserted into the words – for example, innate + car = inCARnate.

1. Farm, sly, mover, sty, flock

2. Try, sing, legs, pant

3. Hung, mars, tone, say

4. Bred, leer, mate, brigs

5. Sane, per, fling, red

6. Wing, tow, bad, fen, show

# NUMBER CODE

R.O.WHITAKER, USA

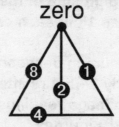

zero

Working from the diagram above, can you decode the following and then say what significant feature the answers have in common?

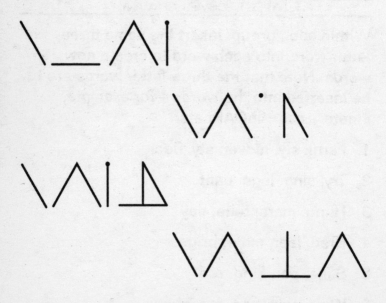

# EINSTEIN

ADAM ALEXIS, UK

Fit the five pieces together in such a way that a quotation by Albert Einstein can be read in a sequential pattern.

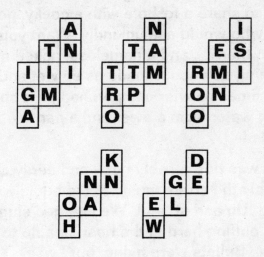

## CONCEALED CREATURES

STEVE PLATER, UK

Hidden in the story below are lots of different living creatures, all commonly known. How many can you find?

## A DRAMATIC ESCAPE

I had spent the night in gale-force winds, forced to share a foxhole with a cocky, poxy fellow who would ask unkindly 'Want your mother, then?', and a nameless, naked man. A teeming downpour made us so wet and my kit ten times heavier as I perched on a board, sipping water from a ewer and a pan the rain filled.

Now it was hot, terribly hot – and eerily quiet. Suddenly the crude music of the bugle was playing 'Up and at 'em!' We charged slug-gishly, puffing hard in the heat, unable to breathe. Bullets were flying, but I was unscathed as I ducked and weaved to and fro, grasping my lucky amulet. I chose my path awkwardly but shrewdly, based on key points of army doctrine.

A gleam caught my eye – a rifle aimed at me. Then a bang. I dove into a hole, landing heavily. The round bounced off my helmet, nicked my thumb and bowled the Lieutenant over. He became limp, a last agonized groan and stench marked his final breath. 'O God, O God!' I cursed, feeling sadder and more anti-war than ever. Why did I sign up for a combat command? It was a bleeding horror, a nightmare. I'd rather be a raw rookie in the sixth (or seventh) battalion, not a hero – a chaplain rather.

That made me pause a little and think of the Gospel. 'I cannot abide more vile murder. I'll go AWOL for a while,' I decided. It was now or, maybe, never. So I fled with the man I liked the most, Richards (Bill), a coy, pure chap, who had also been badly shaken by the carnage. We weren't craven cowards, or cared a cent who thought so. But neither of us wanted to endure what could be a very long war.

We crept through a tunnel, keeping low, to a road. I followed the map I kept in my pigskin pouch. I wished for the car I bought a month ago, a Triumph with new tyres and the famous emblem. No car passed by, so we had to hijack a lorry, then took steerage berths on a boat heading overseas. And so we both rushed to freedom. I had a bout of catarrh, in other respects I'm now hale and far healthier, and my thumb is on the mend. We now rent a cottage away from all the danger, Bill and I, and live in peace studying molecular biology and playing Scrabble.

# THE ANT AND CONE

MEL BEBEE, USA

A cone has a base diameter of 4cm and a slant height of 12cm. An ant is located 5cm from the apex of the cone. What is the minimum distance that the ant will have to travel to circumnavigate the cone and return to its original starting point?

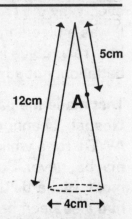

# LIST

LLOYD KING, UK

Here is a list of letters: B, F, H, K, L, P, S. Which of the following letters can also be added to it?

U, V, W, X, Y

# SUM IT

PETER SCHMIES, GERMANY

What number comes next in this series?

495, 440, 639, 296, 273, 174, 185, 42 ?

# CUBE ROUTES

GEOFF HINCHLIFFE, UK

Emperor Hang'sen of the Gindex decreed that a sacred pyramid be built, using cubic blocks in squares of steadily decreasing size, to a single-block apex from which he could worship the mighty Dol-lar each day.

Tradition dictated that the Emperor should ascend from the top of block A to the apex by the shortest possible route, which should be different each day, until all possibilities were exhausted, when he would be sacrificed to the mighty Dol-lar and succeeded by his eldest son.

Each shortest route by which the Emperor can ascend consists of a combination of sideways and upward movements; diagonal movements are not allowed. There are, for example, 6 routes from A to C and 20 routes from A to D.

If Hang'sen's pyramid contained 969 blocks, for how many days did he reign after the pyramid had been built?

## SATELLITES

CHRIS HARDING, AUSTRALIA

Three satellites orbit the moon, passing directly above the heads of two observers at intervals of 5, 25 and 40 hours. Observer A transmits a message to Observer B at the moment he sees all three together in the heavens.

How long must Observer B, who is on a different part of the moon, wait before he, too, is able to find them all together once again and report back his findings to Observer A?

Q62  A35

## TRIANGLES

LLOYD KING, UK

Complete the bottom rectangle.

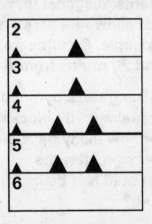

# CODED MESSAGE

AUDREY AUSTIN, AUSTRALIA

Solve the following code:

PIOH SXHMT, ANX NOZN OK MIVOXAF

# EMPTY SQUARES

ADAM ALEXIS, UK

Two squares in this grid have to remain empty.
Fill in the remainder of the grid using the
words listed below. Two of the squares
contain only one word each.

| A | BUYER | CHARM | LA |
|---|---|---|---|
| YAM | | | A |
| BEET | | | |

| | | | |
|---|---|---|---|
| BED | COT | RUN | FAR |
| US | SPERM | CREME | |
| RIP | ROBE | GUT | |
| MOB | NERVE | JAY | |

# G-R-R-RIDDLE 2

MITZI CHRISTIANSEN KUEHL, USA

In the following crossword puzzle a letter or letters occupy the squares to form complete words horizontally and vertically. The number in each square represents the number of letters to be placed in that square – for example, there are two letters in square 1–1.

|   | 1 | 2 | 3 | 4 |
|---|---|---|---|---|
| **1** | ② | ① | ④ | ③ |
| **2** | ① | ① | ④ | ④ |
| **3** | ① | ① | ④ | ④ |
| **4** | ① | ② | ④ | ① |

## Across
1. The winter of our_____
2. Separable by filtration
3. A healing dose or application
4. Exalted spirits

## Down
1. Dime (obsolete form)
2. Inscribed pillar
3. Improper or harmful remedy
4. Platform supporting a statue (plural)

## DOMINOES

DOUG PATTINSON, UK

The numbers in the grid indicate the dots on separate halves of a set of dominoes. Work out the positions of the complete dominoes. There are three slightly differing solutions to find.

| 0 | 5 | 5 | 3 | 2 | 1 | 2 | 1 |
|---|---|---|---|---|---|---|---|
| 0 | 3 | 4 | 5 | 1 | 4 | 6 | 4 |
| 4 | 6 | 5 | 0 | 0 | 4 | 3 | 1 |
| 5 | 4 | 5 | 3 | 2 | 5 | 3 | 6 |
| 6 | 2 | 0 | 1 | 3 | 2 | 6 | 0 |
| 5 | 4 | 3 | 2 | 0 | 4 | 1 | 3 |
| 1 | 2 | 2 | 6 | 6 | 0 | 1 | 6 |

## GROUPS

CHRIS HARDING, AUSTRALIA

Fill in the missing number in the centre of the second numbers square.

```
415  843  954  123  444  081
337  5?7  725  735  404  533
935  812  932  881  444  336
```

# LETTERS

JAMES SHELDON, UK

Which letter is represented by the question mark in this grid?

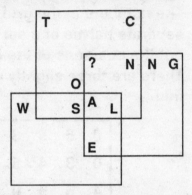

# NUMBERS

CHRIS HARDING, AUSTRALIA

If 99 produces 33, 461 produces 42 and 19 produces 31, what does 961 produce?

# MISSING LETTERS

LLOYD KING, UK

What two letters complete the following?

# I I I V T I I T D I I
# L I L I J I L I D L I

# CRYPTIC WORD SQUARE 2

AUDREY AUSTIN, AUSTRALIA

A 6 x 6 magic word square is one in which the same six words read the same both across and down. The answer to each of the six clues is a six-letter word that, with the other five answers, will form a 6 x 6 word square.

|   | 1 | 2 | 3 | 4 | 5 | 6 |
|---|---|---|---|---|---|---|
| 1 |   |   |   |   |   |   |
| 2 |   |   |   |   |   |   |
| 3 |   |   |   |   |   |   |
| 4 |   |   |   |   |   |   |
| 5 |   |   |   |   |   |   |
| 6 |   |   |   |   |   |   |

## Clues

1. Lymph cured pals by degree.
2. Church in the fight to retain moss.
3. Add string to a broken chain. That's getting smart.
4. Quietly involved with Japanese religion.
5. Term no psychotic a wise counsellor.
6. Yarn or let out a terrible groan.

# ALPHAMETICS 2

MITZI CHRISTIANSEN KUEHL, USA

Substitute numbers for letters in the following
calculations. The question marks and Xs in
both puzzles represent letters that do not
appear in the body of the problem.

1.
```
                          I Q
              ------
HIGH / I RONIC
              HIGH
              ----
              ONRXC
              ONCXC
              -----
                X ? ?
```

2.
```
                             TEN
                  --------
CARTER / FEENSTRA
                  EXRFRC
                  ------
                  X?TSRCR
                  XSC?EST
                  -------
                  XXETNFA
                  XAX?TXN
                  --------
                  XS?X?N
```

## PROVERB ANAGRAMS

STEVE PLATER, UK

Each of the following is an anagram of a familiar proverb. Can you solve them?

1. I rise to change my bath.
2. Fourteen others show Mike it.
3. Strive to buy wet fish oil.
4. On Monday eat a pear, fish or noodles.
5. I fell on the other banana fast.

## A CALENDAR QUIZ

KENT L.ALDERSHOF, USA

1. What boy's name is embedded in successive months? What does the calendar imply is his vocation?
2. What unisex name is embedded in the calendar?
3. What is the golden month?
4. What is the iron month?
5. What is the moon month?
6. What is the radioactive month?

# FAIRY FOOTPRINTS

BOB NEWMAN, UK

'Fairy chess' is the phrase used to describe any non-standard form of the game. Many weird and wonderful pieces have been invented, usually with moves derived, with a little imagination, from those of the normal chess pieces.

Each of the diagrams shows a normal chess board with the positions of four pieces marked. Each diagram relates to a different fairy piece, and the marked squares are four to which it could move from its present position. Can you deduce on which square the piece stands, describe its move and, perhaps, suggest a name for it?

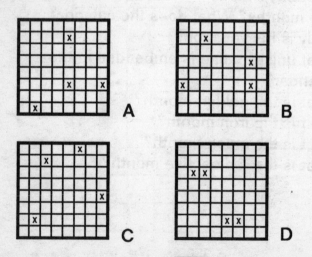

# ASSEMBLAGES

TONY LAYTON, UK

Find the collective names for the following and fit them in to the grid. The first answer has already been inserted.

1. A _____ of guns
2. A _____ of beer
3. A _____ of kine
4. A _____ of oxen
5. A _____ of bucks
6. A _____ of toads
7. A _____ of trees
8. A _____ of geese
9. A _____ of hawks
10. A _____ of saints
11. A _____ of grouse
12. A _____ of horses
13. A _____ of widgeon
14. A _____ of dunlin
15. A _____ of peacocks
16. A _____ of leopards
17. A _____ of bitterns
18. A _____ of giraffes
19. A _____ of kangaroos

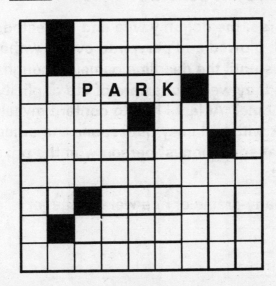

# GRAIN OF TRUTH

RAY WILBUR, USA

Some time ago, a local store held a contest, offering a prize to whoever should make the most accurate estimate of the quantity of grains of rice in a large jar in its window.

By accident, I learned the answer but kept it to myself out of greed, in expectation of winning the contest. However the answer was stated in a way that was cryptic, at least to me. It read: 'The quantity of grains of rice in the jar is the sum of all the cubes from 1 up to and including a certain number, which exceeds the square root of the square root of that sum by 40 per cent.'

The horse, the dog, my wife and I sweated, panted, glowed and perspired over it without success until the deadline came (although, to be fair, they were not aware of the duplicity of my scheme). At last I had to content myself in despair with a clumsy guess, and the outcome was that some honest person won the prize instead.

How many grains of rice were in the jar?

# SEQUENCE

AUDREY AUSTIN, AUSTRALIA

Complete this sequence.

24, 15, 27, 57 ?

# SYMBOLS

LLOYD KING, UK

Choose one of the six symbols below to complete this grid

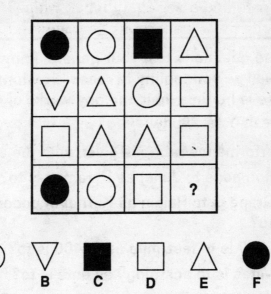

A    B    C    D    E    F

# THE MAGIC CUBE

CHRIS HARDING, AUSTRALIA

A magic 'cube' has seven dimensions, of which your vision can detect only four. Each side is made up of nine square blocks. Each of these is coloured red when it is visible. The rest are white. How many white surface squares formed from the blocks are there if only the four dimensional blocks may be rotated for extended viewing?

# ANALOGIES

PETER SCHMIES, GERMANY

These questions test your general knowledge as well as your ability to research information. There is no time limit and any works of reference may be consulted.

A performance rating is given with the answer.

1. Romeo is to Juliet as Pyramus is to?

2. Grape is to Raisin as Kernel of coconut is to?

3. 5280 is to feet/mile as 86400 is to?

4. Mites is to acarology as ants is to?

5. Wood is to Dryad as mountain is to?

6. Empty hand is to karate as divine wind is to?

7. 100 is to Sleeping Beauty as 20 is to?

8. Lions is to pride as leopards is to?

9. Widespread is to epidemic as localized is to?

10. Alpha is to Beta as Dubhe is to?

11. Norway is to Storting as Iceland is to?

12. Pneumatic tyre is to Dunlop as parking meter is to?

13. Laurel-tree is to Daphne as reed is to?

14. Trochee is to iambus as N is to?

15. Guanine is to cytosine as thymine is to?

16. Third is to tritagonist as second is to?

17. Hercule Poirot is to Hastings as Nero Wolfe is to?

18. Salmon is to Anadromous as eel is to?

19. Sklodowska is to Curie as Grosholtz is to?

20. Whole is to part as Holo- is to?

21. Short is to myopia as normal is to?

22. Corsica is to Maquis as California is to?

23. -18 is to atto- as 18 is to?

24. Lift is to elevator as vest is to?

25. Dog is to canine as weasel is to?

# GRID

LLOYD KING, UK

Find the missing number.

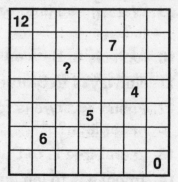

# THE COIL

MEL BEBEE, USA

As an engineer, I want to construct a special inductor on a coil form 3cm in circumference. My calculations indicate that I will need a coil of eight turns evenly spaced over a length of 7cm. What is the total length of the wire used?

**Eight turns evenly spaced**

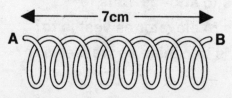

**Coil form 3cm in circumference**

# WORDS WITHIN WORDS

BILL KUEHL, USA

Some words swallow others – for example, the answer to the clue 'packaged rodent' would be cRATe. Find the animals described by the following.

1. Small mammal gobbles big bird.
2. Bird tied up in searching investigation.
3. Delicate creature ends up in feast.
4. Steed surrounded by a founder.
5. Tapped in, not out.
6. Tamed by fighter.
7. Bird overcome by frowns.
8. Monkish viper.
9. Nimble animal caught up by chance.
10. Legendary bird not to be believed?
11. Nocturnal beast given back.
12. Pretty bird sorrows.
13. Friendly pet spread about.
14. Carefree animal divides possessions.
15. Big animal shows restraint.

# PLAYFAIR

BOB NEWMAN, UK

Playfair codes are a cruel and unusual form of punishment that sometimes appear in insanely difficult crossword puzzles. The code depends on a keyword of which all the letters must be different. This keyword is written in a 5 x 5 square, followed by the remaining letters of the alphabet in order, I and J are treated as the same letter. Letters of the message can then be encoded in pairs. If the two letters are the same or are in the same row, each maps to the letter immediately to the right (the last letter in the row mapping to the first). If the two letters are in the same column, each maps to the letter immediately below (the bottom letter mapping to the topmost one). If the two letters appear as diagonally opposite corners of a rectangle, they encode to the letters at the other two corners, as if the rectangle were reflected in a vertical axis. For example, if the keyword were HANDIWORK, the square would be:

```
H  A  N  D  I
W  O  R  K  B
C  E  F  G  L
M  P  Q  S  T
U  V  X  Y  Z
```

and the word BATTLE, for example, would encode to OIMMCF.

Playfair codes in general are extremely difficult to crack, but try this one. The message is not a well-known quotation, but a simple sentence composed with solubility in mind. If you can't get started, don't like the encoded form of the message or can't guess the keyword, just remember it's not my fault, OK? Here's the message:

QW BIZALQOIU NXOZALQZ PQ

FUX-LMXPK THL LTGGXX, IPGGXX

QOAAEX, PBN TYPITEMOP.

# ANAGRAMS

CHRIS HARDING, AUSTRALIA

When they are assembled, the following will make you a whole person:

DCSEYNEAHKEE NTKUR RGAMLESS ANDHESETF

# LETTERS

JAMES SHELDON, UK

Which letter should be in place of the question mark in the following sequence?

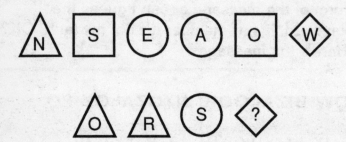

# POTATOES

KEVIN N. STONE, UK

A farmer has 7,031 potatoes, which he has to put into sacks. All the sacks must contain the same number of potatoes, and the farmer should use as few sacks as possible. How many potatoes does he put into how many sacks?

# SOMETHING IN COMMON

LLOYD KING, UK

What have all of these words in common?

VEAL
LOFT
SEW
SIN

# ALPHABET CROSSWORD 2

AUDREY AUSTIN, AUSTRALIA

Using all 26 letters of the alphabet, once each only, fill in the blanks to complete the crossword with good English words.

| | A | | M | | |
| | N | | A | | E |
| | I | E | R | | T |
| M | E | | | I | |
| S | | S | E | | |
| | I | T | | | |
| I | | | I | O | U |
| E | R | | L | | |
| | | T | R | E | S |

A B C D
E F G H
I J K L
M N O P
Q R S T
U V W X
Y Z

# CONTAINER

MITZI CHRISTIANSEN KUEHL, USA

In a container one or more short words are contained within a longer word. The word seafarer, for example, contains the words seer and afar – se(afar)er.

1.  What is so rare as the month of MMM,
    If I MMM paraphrase?
    Now is the time for romantic eves
    And heady, balmy days.

    MMM is the month a strange MM%%%M
    Confounds a %%% and lass
    Mindlessly courting some phantasy
    And cutting every class.

2.  In those nostalgic days of yore
    When we were on the ZZZZ,
    I'd gather rejects at the store
    And make a casserole.

    A dish made up of scrap and scrimp,
    Of humbler porker snouts,
    An onion soiled, a carrot limp,
    Potatoes that had sprouts.

    But with home brew, Oh! What impact!
    A dish so XXZZZZXX
    It helped us overlook the fact
    We couldn't pay the XXXX.

# MISSING NUMBER

LLOYD KING, UK

Find the missing number.

| URN | 49 |
| NET | 92 |
| VET | 52 |
| WOO | ? |

# SORE THUMBS

BOB NEWMAN, UK

Identify the odd one out in each of the following groups.

1. Animal, creature, dog, live, rat
2. Art, chained, design, toga, orchestra
3. Begin, chop, crux, floppy, wrong
4. Boracic, kill, quaver, undercoat, view
5. Broad, gain, mass, oology, wash
6. Canine, maintenance, relevant, semitone, weight
7. Chandler, embrace, investment, socket, tollbooth
8. Channel, cook, hostile, sandwich, society
9. Complex, frequent, occasional, wretched, zebra
10. First, somnolent, spontaneous, studious, undefiled

# FIVE BY FIVE

MITZI CHRISTIANSEN KUEHL, USA

Assign numbers to the letters of the alphabet – A=1, B=2...Z=26 – to solve the following 5 x 5 word square. The answers are all five-letter words that, when placed correctly in the grid, can be read both horizontally and vertically. One word is repeated.

## Clues

A four-square palindromic belief. Run off with Richard. Banishment!

|  |  |  |  |  | = 64 |
|--|--|--|--|--|------|
|  |  |  |  |  | = 55 |
|  |  |  |  |  | = 76 |
|  |  |  |  |  | = 53 |
|  |  |  |  |  | = 64 |

# GEOGRANNY

### JAMES HARBECK, CANADA

The name of this puzzle, for those who are wondering, is composite of 'geography' and 'anagram'.

The following bizarre rhyme is composed of the 26 anagrammed names of geographical features, one after another. All the places in the poem have something in common. The title of the poem is a hint – it is not part of the puzzle. The spacing and punctuation of the verse are irrelevant to the solution.

Can you work out the names and what they have in common?

### Friends of Mr Cairo
'Melon jam and eel, vile rib lard...
Akbar, goon eater – or pig –,
Will Eno cork any gas-riled sumo?'
'Ah, give a razz, Bill, babe,
man is a bus – big'
'Unawed oink, hash in a skin,
boar, I slog at a bar,
and you ease rum and luau in.' Stop!
It riles as a drama, lout:
I bid, jump to a car.
                              – A.C.

# THE AUTOMOBILE

PETER SCHMIES, GERMANY

Add four straight lines, about the same length as those shown, to get a car.

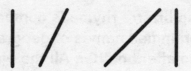

# SOMETHING IN COMMON

LLOYD KING, UK

What have all of these words in common?

CLING
DRIVE
FORT
MOTION
STATE

# ANSWERS

Bullbat (10), Lark (10.5), Ptarmigan (11), Dove (11.5), Quail (12), Starling (12.5) and Peewit (13). Taking A = 1, B = 2, and so on, divide the sum of the letters in each word by the number of letters in that word to obtain a sequence from 10 to 13, ascending in intervals of 0.5.

| A2 | **CUBE ROUTES** | Q60 |
| --- | --- | --- |

The number of blocks in such pyramids, counting from the top, is 1 + 9 + 25 + 49 + ... i.e.,

$$\sum(2m-1)^2$$

when $m$ is the number of layers. Since $969 = 1^2 + 3^2 + 5^2 \dots + 17^2$, there are nine layers.

In Hang'sen's ascent the bottom layer is assumed as already mounted, so he climbs eight layers. If $n$ is the number of layers to be climbed, the number of routes is the middle term of the $(2*n)$th line in Pascal's triangle. In our case, $n = 8$; therefore there are

$$\frac{16!}{8!8!} = 12,870$$

possible routes. So Hang'sen continued to reign for *12,870* days – i.e., more than 35 years – after the pyramid had been built.

This is essentially the same as finding the number of routes from one corner of a chessboard to the opposite diagonal corner, always moving positively.

| A3 | **SHORT LIST** | Q3 |
| --- | --- | --- |

Dell: if you look at the lower case letters and those without ascenders (i.e., o, m, z and so on) you will see a list of colours running through the words – maroon, cream, mauve and rose.

| A4 | TOILETS OUT OF ORDER | Q29 |
| --- | --- | --- |

The poet is T.S. Eliot. The quotes are:

Oh, do not ask, 'what is it?'
Let us go and make our visit.

*The Love Song of J. Alfred Prufrock*

The worlds revolve like ancient women
Gathering fuel in vacant lots.

*Preludes, IV*

Unreal City,
Under the brown fog of a winter dawn.

*The Wasteland, I*

This is the way the world ends
Not with a bang but a whimper.

*The Hollow Men, V*

I should be glad of another death.

*Journey of the Magi*

| A5 | LETTERS | Q68 |
| --- | --- | --- |

D: the three boxes contain the letters of Scotland, England and Wales.

| A6 | ANAGRAMS | Q86 |
| --- | --- | --- |

Eyes, Head, Neck; Trunk; Arms, Legs; Feet, Hands

| A7 | SORE THUMBS | Q93 |
| --- | --- | --- |

1. Creature – the other words form new words when reversed; 2. Design – the others are anagrams of animals (rat, echidna, goat and carthorse); 3. Wrong – the letters of the other words are in alphabetical order; 4. Undercoat – the last letter of the other words is the successor to the first letter; 5. Oology – the other words form new words when preceded by a- (abroad, again, amass and awash); 6. Relevant – the other words contain hidden numbers; 7. Chandler – the other words contain hidden clothing; 8. Hostile – the other words are the names of islands; 9. Frequent – in the other words the first and last letters are placed symmetrically in the alphabet; 10. Spontaneous – the other words contain three consecutive letters of the alphabet.

| A8 | NUMBER CODE | Q54 |
|---|---|---|

They are all dates connected with feats of achievement and exploration: 1492 (Columbus), 1903 (Wright), 1927 (Lindbergh), 1969 (Armstrong).

| A9 | SPOTS BEFORE YOUR EYES | Q35 |
|---|---|---|

Nothing: the circles contain views of the eight corners of a die.

| A10 | THE FENCE | Q15 |
|---|---|---|

This question requires a little lateral thinking. The only requirement is to divide the field equally with the minimum fence. The first reaction is to try the various vertical, horizontal and diagonal solutions. I offer the challenge that the minimum length is the arc of a circle.

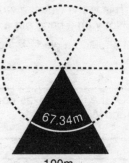

67.34m

100m

Given the dimensions, it is easy to calculate the area of the field and one half of that amount. The latter value represents a sector one-sixth of a circle.

It is now easy to calculate the circle and its main parameters, including the circumference. One-sixth of the circumference is the length of the fence – a little under 67.34 metres.

| A11 | BATH PUZZLE | Q26 |
|---|---|---|

8 minutes: $(9^{-1} + 24^{-1} - 36^{-1})^{-1}$ *Note: $9^{-1}=\frac{1}{9}$ (reciprocal)*

| A12 | TRIPLE PLAY PUZZLES | Q43 |
|---|---|---|

The.Cat and the Rat: 1. cathedrals, rationally; 2. scathingly, fratricide; 3. decathlon, paratroops; 4. avocations, ungrateful; 5. caricature, decorators; 6. obfuscates, dehydrated; 7. adjudicate, plutocrats; 8. requiescat, bureaucrat.

The Oriental Treasures: Her cloisonnes: 1. dehumidification, 2. overcompensation, 3. christianization, 4. declassification, 5. collectivization, 6. photocomposition, 7. reinterpretation, 8. mispronunciation, 9. pro-desegregation, 10. non-proliferation, 11. contraindication, 12. predetermination, 13. disqualification.

2: for each square total the digits in the corners, then total the remaining numbers – i.e., those in the centre of each side. The number in the centre of each square is the square root of the difference between the two totals.

1.

$$\begin{array}{r} 17 \\ \hline 9189/156413 \\ 9189 \\ \hline 64523 \\ 64323 \\ \hline 200 \end{array}$$

2.

$$\begin{array}{r} 485 \\ \hline 203483/98856430 \\ 813932 \\ \hline 1746323 \\ 1627864 \\ \hline 1184590 \\ 1017415 \\ \hline 167175 \end{array}$$

21: the first two letters in each word are the last two letters of the first number in the following number and the last letter is the first letter of the second number – for example, foUR Nine = 49.

If you pronounce the first letter of each word as an individual syllable you get a new word.

Albion Theatre/Presents/Hamlet on stage/Each night – ten sharp/(Not Easter Monday)/Star: Charles Darwin/Starlet: Ingrid Turpin/Producer: Dennis Davies/Director: Ingmar Andrews/Prices from three thousand lira

E: substitute each symbol in the grid for the appropriate letter from the row of symbols below the grid to find four four-letter words reading across.

| A19 | KEYWORDS | Q5 |

1. Quinquereme, 2. Rejoinder, 3. Inquire, 4. Fasten,
5. Understaffed, 6. Yankee, 7. Kayak, 8. Pillow, 9. Expire,
10. Overdid, 11. Thank, 12. Jazzy, 13. Lorimer,
14. Spearmint, 15. Aghast, 16. Zenana, 17. Deprivation,
18. Velocipede, 19. Xebec, 20. Cribbed, 21. Gantries,
22. Bromide, 23. Hydrangea, 24. Mixer, 25. Natterjack,
26. Willow.

| A20 | A WORD QUIZ | Q8 |

Each one forms another ordinary word, with a different meaning, by the addition of the same initial letter, F.

| FABLE | FEELS | FLAWS | FLOUT | FRANK |
| FACED | FEWER | FLAYS | FLOWS | FRAYS |
| FACES | FIRES | FLEAS | FLUFF | FREED |
| FAILS | FLAGS | FLEER | FLUKE | FRILL |
| FAINT | FLAIR | FLEES | FOILS | FRISK |
| FAIRS | FLAKE | FLICK | FOLIO | FRITZ |
| FARMS | FLAME | FLIES | FOURS | FROCK |
| FEARS | FLANK | FLINT | FOWLS | FRUMP |
| FEAST | FLAPS | FLIPS | FRAGS | FUSED |
| FEATS | FLASH | FLOGS | FRAIL | FUSES |

| A21 | FOUR-LETTER WORDS | Q12 |

Nose: all the others are French words that are, in some way, related to the human body; dent = tooth, main = hand, pied = foot, rein = kidney and ride = wrinkle. They also, of course, happen to be English words with 'non-body' meanings. Nose is an English word only; it means nothing in French.

| B | A | S | I | C | S |
|---|---|---|---|---|---|
| A | L | I | G | H | T |
| S | I | G | N | O | R |
| I | G | N | O | R | E |
| C | H | O | R | E | S |
| S | T | R | E | S | S |

---

## A23      THINK TWICE BEFORE YOU LEAP      Q49

37: the sequence consists of two alternating series –
17 (+2=), 19 (+3=), 22 (+4=), 26 (+5=), 31 (+6=), 37; and
18 (+2=), 20 (+4=), 24 (+6=), 30 (+8=), 38.

---

## A24      DOMINOES      Q66

| 0 | 5 | 5 | 3 | 2 | 1 | 2 | 1 |
|---|---|---|---|---|---|---|---|
| 0 | 3 | 4 | 5 | 1 | 4 | 6 | 4 |
| 4 | 6 | 5 | 0 | 0 | 4 | 3 | 1 |
| 5 | 4 | 5 | 3 | 2 | 5 | 3 | 6 |
| 6 | 2 | 0 | 1 | 3 | 2 | 6 | 0 |
| 5 | 4 | 3 | 2 | 0 | 4 | 1 | 3 |
| 1 | 2 | 2 | 6 | 6 | 0 | 1 | 6 |

---

## A25      CODED MESSAGE      Q63

Join Mensa, the High IQ Society (Code: A = T, B = U, C = V,
D = W, E = X, F = Y, G = Z, H = N, I = O, J = P, K = Q, L = R,
M = S and so on)

---

## A26      ANAGRAMS      Q42

1. Oxford English Dictionary; 2. Not worth a damn;
3. Hypocorism; 4. The United States Boomerang Association

| A27 | GEOGRANNY | Q95 |
| --- | --- | --- |

They are capital cities in Africa – Lome, N'djamena, Libreville, Dakar, Gaborone, Pretoria, Lilongwe, Conakry, Algiers, Mogadishu, Brazzaville, Mbabane, Windhoek, Kinshasa, Nairobi, Lagos, Rabat, Yaounde, Maseru, Luanda, Tunis, Tripoli, Dar es Salaam, Djibouti, Maputo, Accra

| A28 | ANALOGIES | Q81 |
| --- | --- | --- |

1. Thisbe; 2. Copra; 3. Seconds/day; 4. Myrmecology; 5. Oread; 6. Kamikaze; 7. Rip Van Winkle; 8. Leap (collective name); 9. Endemic; 10. Merak (stars in the Great Bear); 11. Althing; 12. Magee; 13. Syrinx; 14. A (corresponds to short/long in the Morse Code); 15. Adenine (in DNA); 16. Deuteragonist; 17. Goodwin; 18. Catadromous; 19. Tussaud; 20. Mero-; 21. Emmetropia; 22. Chaparral; 23. Exa-; 24. Undershirt; 25. Musteline

Rating: 4-6 average; 7-10 good; 11-14 very good; 15-18 excellent; 19-24 exceptional; 25 superbrain

| A29 | MISSING LETTERS | Q7 |
| --- | --- | --- |

UCAN: the whole sentence is simply a list of birds – i.e., kiwi, stork, rhea, swan, ibis, toucan.

| A30 | ALPHABET CROSSWORD 1 | Q16 |
| --- | --- | --- |

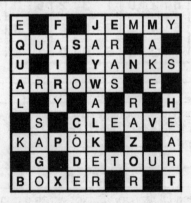

Representatives, Sententiousness

Avail. Delete the first letter, then subsequent alternate letters to reveal consecutive Roman numerals: Dig (i), Minim (ii), Militia (iii), Sieve (iv), Ave (v), Avail (vi)

| A JAY RUN | BUYER FAR | CHARM | LA RIP |
|---|---|---|---|
| YAM | | | A US GUT |
| BEET SPERM | COT ROBE | MOB NERVE | BED CREME |

These are all anagrams of months of the year.

| JANUARY | FEBRUARY | MARCH | APRIL |
|---|---|---|---|
| MAY | | | AUGUST |
| SEPTEMBER | OCTOBER | NOVEMBER | DECEMBER |

25cm: lay the coil on a flat plane and attach point A. Unroll the coil eight turns, which will be 24 cm. During that time the wire will move 7cm to the right. The resulting hypotenuse of the right-angled triangle is the length of the wire – i.e., 25cm.

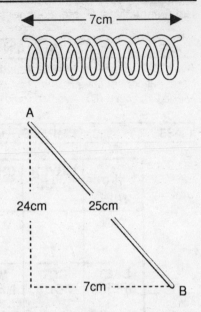

It is the 2, 3, 4, 5 and 6 of diamonds from a pack of cards placed on top of each other.

1. 5: the series consists of the first digits of the number *pi* (3.1415926...), but 1 has been subtracted from each digit.

2. 1: the sequence is based on the digits in the number *pi* (3.1415926535), with 1 indicating an odd digit and 0 indicating an even digit.

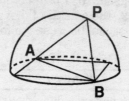

Any triangle, such as ABP, being right-angled, gives a Pythagorean triple with a hypotenuse of 65. Only four integral solutions exist – i.e., (16, 63, 65), (25, 60, 65), (39, 52, 65), and (33, 56, 65), of which the last two satisfy the condition of totalling 180 metres:

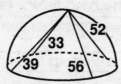

---

1. February, fury, bare; 2. angrier, rearing, earring; 3. a, sport, cat, catastrophe, he; 4. armchair, air, March; 5. dowager, wordage; 6. Billingsgate, gin, bilge, salt; 7. December, embers, kin, Dickens; 8. grim, lens, gremlins; 9. cautioned, auctioned, education; 10. juvenile, June, live; 11. bordello doorbell.

---

1. Ca/Nadia/n; 2. Ca/Stella/n; 3. Ca/Tamara/n

---

| T | E | N | E | T |
|---|---|---|---|---|
| E | X | I | L | E |
| N | I | X | O | N |
| E | L | O | P | E |
| T | E | N | E | T |

| A41 | POTATOES | Q88 |
|---|---|---|

89 potatoes in 79 sacks: 7,031 is the product of two prime numbers – 79 and 89. The smaller of these two numbers has to be the number of sacks, because the farmer should use as few sacks as possible.

| A42 | NUMBERS | Q69 |
|---|---|---|

43: a number is produced by writing down the number preceding it backwards, breaking down the results into obvious subgroups and then taking the square root of these subgroups – 961 → 169, the square root of 16 is 4, and the square root of 9 is 3.

| A43 | TRADING PUNCHES | Q51 |
|---|---|---|

20 : 9 favouring Angela: ((5*.2)*1/(1.5))/(3*.1)

| A44 | GRANDAD'S AGE | Q47 |
|---|---|---|

He was born in 1892, and he was 44 in 1936.

| A45 | QUOTATION | Q41 |
|---|---|---|

You can fool some of the people all of the time and all of the people some of the time, but you can't fool all of the people all of the time.

| A46 | APARTMENT BLOCKS | Q23 |
|---|---|---|

The white windows in the apartments form the numbers 2, 3, 4 and 5. Therefore, these windows should be black to give the number 6.

| A47 | RESERVES | Q34 |
|---|---|---|

13.5 minutes: (15 x 36) ÷ 40

| A48 | SCREEN SCRAMBLE | Q14 |
|---|---|---|

1. *Rain Man* – Dustin Hoffman, Tom Cruise;
2. *From Russia with Love* – Sean Connery;
3. *The China Syndrome* – Jane Fonda

| A49 | THE AUTOMOBILE | Q96 |
|---|---|---|

| A50 | THE ANT AND THE CONE | Q57 |
|---|---|---|

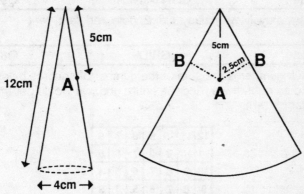

The first point is to recognize that this can be changed from a three-dimensional problem to one of two dimensions. At the point opposite the ant, cut the cone from base to apex and lay it out flat. It forms a sector of a circle with an apex angle of 60 degrees.

From the point where the ant starts, its shortest distance to the cut edge is point B (the perpendicular). Since this is a right triangle with angles 30-60-90, the distance from ant to point B is one-half the distance of ant to apex, or 2.5cm

On the opposite side of the sector is shown another point B. If the cone is re-assembled, it will be seen that these are both the same point.

So the ant re-appears at the second point B and again travels 2.5cm to home. Total travel distance is 5cm.

| A51 | LETTER CHANGE | Q38 |
| --- | --- | --- |

1. suspicious, auspicious; 2. abused, amused; 3. friction, fraction; 4. denial, venial; 5. status, statue; 6. certain, curtain

| A52 | PROVERB ANAGRAMS | Q73 |
| --- | --- | --- |

1. Charity begins at home. 2. There's no smoke without fire; 3. Brevity is the soul of wit; 4. A fool and his money are soon parted; 5. Half a loaf is better than none

| A53 | SOMETHING IN COMMON | Q89 |
| --- | --- | --- |

They are all contained in the question.

| A54 | CONTAINER | Q91 |
| --- | --- | --- |

1. May, may, May, malady, lad; 2. dole, redolent, rent

| A55 | GRID | Q82 |
| --- | --- | --- |

8: each number is the sum of the number of squares below it and to its right. If we filled the entire grid, we would get this regular pattern:

| 12 | 11 | 10 | 9 | 8 | 7 | 6 |
| --- | --- | --- | --- | --- | --- | --- |
| 11 | 10 | 9 | 8 | 7 | 6 | 5 |
| 10 | 9 | 8 | 7 | 6 | 5 | 4 |
| 9 | 8 | 7 | 6 | 5 | 4 | 3 |
| 8 | 7 | 6 | 5 | 4 | 3 | 2 |
| 7 | 6 | 5 | 4 | 3 | 2 | 1 |
| 6 | 5 | 4 | 3 | 2 | 1 | 0 |

| A56 | ACROSTIC 2 | Q45 |
| --- | --- | --- |

The judicial power ought to be distinct from both the legislative and executive and independent upon both so that it may be a check upon both. (*Thoughts*, John Adams)

1. Japonica; 2. Obbligato; 3. Hottentot; 4. Nephew; 5. Addendum; 6. Dunce; 7. Anvil, 8. Minions; 9. Schipperke; 10. Theft; 11. Hoch; 12. Octave; 13. Ubiety; 14. Gabbro, 15. Hittite; 16. Tuxedoed; 19. Shuttle

| A57 | PROVERB | Q4 |
|---|---|---|

You cannot make an omelette without breaking eggs.

| A58 | DETECTIVE WORK | Q24 |
|---|---|---|

Eddie

| A59 | WHERE'S MY HOME? | Q30 |
|---|---|---|

City: just add -city to the end of each place named.

| A60 | REBUSES | Q17 |
|---|---|---|

March, w(in)d; W(in)d; Hu(mid)ity; March; Th(under)head

| A61 | WORDS | Q50 |
|---|---|---|

4: the end of the word in the second box, followed by the beginning of the word in the first box creates a new word, which can be preceded by the word in the ellipse – Secret stAG ENTrance, Trade stUN IONize and Ballet seDAN CEReal.

| A62 | MISSING LETTERS | Q70 |
|---|---|---|

D completes the top row, and I completes the bottom row. Joined together, the two sequences form the words LILY, JILT and BLIP.

| A63 | ALPHABET CROSSWORD 2 | Q90 |
|---|---|---|

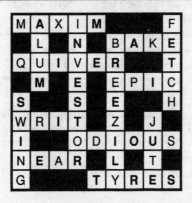

12,642: ((6 x (3 to the 7th power)) minus (((3 to the 4th power)-1) x 6))

53: the sum of the divisors – excluding 1 and number itself – of the previous number.

| 24 | 6 | 12 | 5 | 18 |
|----|----|----|----|----|
| 13 | 10 | 17 | 9 | 16 |
| 11 | 7 | 1 | 25 | 21 |
| 3 | 23 | 15 | 22 | 2 |
| 14 | 19 | 20 | 4 | 8 |

| 17 | 5 | 10 | 20 | 13 |
|----|----|----|----|----|
| 16 | 23 | 14 | 8 | 4 |
| 11 | 7 | 1 | 25 | 21 |
| 2 | 24 | 18 | 9 | 12 |
| 19 | 6 | 22 | 3 | 15 |

The problem can be solved in three stages.

1. Identify and list all possible combinations of three cards, such that no two of them occur together in any of the answers submitted by the teams. It will be found that there are 11 such combinations.

2. For each combination, identify the three teams who would have no cards right at all in their submitted answers, should the combination concerned be the correct solution. Add together their team numbers.

3. The solution required must be the one for which these three numbers total twenty, and it will be found that the combination Jack of Spades, Jack of Hearts, King of Diamonds uniquely meets this requirement. This is, therefore, the correct solution.

The question itself must be something along the lines of: 'Which three of the court cards in a standard pack appear with their faces shown in profile, and are commonly referred to as the "one-eyed cards"?' This is a piece of general knowledge, but anyone unaware of it could no doubt quickly check simply by examining a pack of cards.

**SYNONYM TEST** Q6

1. Principle, principal; 2. Left, deft; 3. Protégé, prodigy, progeny; 4. Defray, affray; 5. Affect, effect; 6. Allude, elude, illude; 7. Desorb, absorb, adsorb; 8. Illicit, elicit; 9. Venal, venial; 10. Deprecate, depreciate; 11. Compliment, complement; 12. Antithesis, prosthesis, synthesis, prothesis

Rating: 4–5 fair; 6–7 good; 8–9 very good; 10–11 excellent; 12 exceptional

---

**A69** **ICEBREAKER** Q32

Mark: the message reads 'Question Mark Willoughby. I am certain he broke your window.'

---

**A70** **PALINDROMIC ROMANCE** Q52

The starting mileage was 12921; the finish mileage was 13731. Ned drove the middle 270 miles at 45mph and the rest of his journey at 30mph.

---

**A71** **FAIRY FOOTPRINTS** Q75

1. Nightrider on D5 – the Nightrider makes one or more knight's moves in the same direction; 2. Camel on D4 – the Camel's move is like a knight's move but one square longer; 3. Archbishop on D2, B4, G5 or E7 – the Archbishop moves like a conventional bishop but can 'bounce' off the edges of the board, although they must remain on squares of the same colour; 4. Princess on D4 – the Princess combines the moves of the knight and the bishop

---

**A72** **LETTERS** Q87

E: letters in triangles spell North; letters in squares spell South; letters in circles spell East; and letters in diamonds spell West.

---

**A73** **AWESOME ANAGRAMS** Q37

1. Those fresh pineapples; 2. The ten digits come; 3. Find mainly rare books; 4. He tended the broken arm; 5. I compete in those set; 6. It must be a sorry tale; 7. Our human genome; 8. This is a dour try in memory search

## A74 EINSTEIN Q55

Imagination is more important than knowledge.

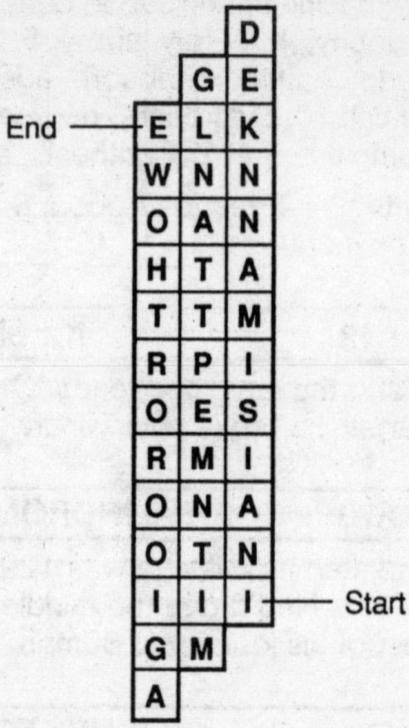


## A75 GRAIN OF TRUTH Q77

1,500,625 grains of rice. The sum of the cubes up to and including $n$ is:

$$\frac{n^2 * (n+1)^2}{4}$$

Let the total number of grains be $g$, and let the square root of the square root of $g$ be $r$ – i.e., $g^{1/4} = r$. We have been told that the 'certain number' $n$ exceeds $r$ by 40 per cent, i.e., $n + 1.4 * r$. We can then say:

$$\left(\frac{(1.4r)^2 * (1.4r+1)^2}{4}\right)^{1/4} = r$$

Solving for $r$ we get: $0.04r^2 - 1.4r = 0$ – i.e., $0.04r = 1.4$, so $r = 35$; therefore $n = 49$ and $g = 1,500,625$.

## A76 SEQUENCES Q18

E, G, W, Y, K, M: these letters complete two sequences that may be read off any standard QWERTY keyboard by reading each second letter.

|   | 1 | 2 | 3 | 4 |
|---|---|---|---|---|
| 1 | DI | S | CONT | ENT |
| 2 | S | T | RAIN | ABLE |
| 3 | M | E | DICA | MENT |
| 4 | E | LA | TION | S |

---

| A78 | | Q61 |
|---|---|---|

66 hours 40 minutes: this reduces to 1, 5 and 8 –
((8*5)/(8–5))*5

---

| A79 | SUM AND PRODUCT | Q10 |
|---|---|---|

£1.20, £1.25, £1.50 and £3.16

---

| A80 | A CALENDAR QUIZ | Q74 |
|---|---|---|

1. Jason (the initial letters of July, August, September, October, November), who is apparently a radio disc jockey – Jason DJ FM-AM (from the initial letters of December, January, February, March, April, May); 2. Jan (JANuary); 3. August (AU = gold); 4. February (FE = iron); 5. September (SE = selenium and Selene is the Greek goddess of the moon): 6. November (NO = nobelium, an artificial radioactive element named after Alfred Nobel, the founder of the Nobel prizes)

---

| A81 | WORDS WITHIN WORDS | Q84 |
|---|---|---|

1. L(emu)r, 2. P(robin)g, 3. C(lamb)ake, 4. E(pony)m,
5. S(pig)ot, 6. B(ox)er, 7. Sc(owl)s, 8. R(asp)utin, 9. L(otter)y,
10. C(roc)k, 11. Re(bat)e, 12. R(egret)s, 13. S(cat)ter,
14. S(hare)s, 15. For(bear)ance.

| P | L | A | S | M | A |
|---|---|---|---|---|---|
| L | I | C | H | E | N |
| A | C | H | I | N | G |
| S | H | I | N | T | O |
| M | E | N | T | O | R |
| A | N | G | O | R | A |

---

## A83     INSERTIONS     Q53

1. Ore (fOREarm, sOREly, mOREover, stOREy, fORElock);
2. End (trENDy, sENDing, legENDs, pENDant); 3. Tin
(hunTINg, marTINs, tonTINe, saTINy); 4. And (brANDed,
leANDer, mANDate, brigANDs); 5. out (sOUTane, pOUTer,
flOUTing, rOUTed); 6. All (wALLing, tALLow, bALLad,
fALLen, shALLow)

---

## A84     ALPHAMETICS 1     Q36

The first pair of answers is:

```
    80947            80945
  + 81945          + 81947
  -------          -------
   162892           162892
```

The second pair is:

```
    79368            79362
  + 71362          + 71368
  -------          -------
   150730           150730
```

---

## A85     THE UNRELIABLE CLOCK     Q39

1.00pm

---

## A86     CHARADES     Q28

1. tile, vice versa, vice, versatile; 2. 'Tis, tissue, sue, issue;

My favourite flavours of ice-cream are coffee, toffee ripple and pistachio. Keyword: EXCULPATION.

| T | E | M | P | T |
|---|---|---|---|---|
| E | X | I | L | E |
| M | I | N | O | R |
| P | L | O | T | S |
| T | E | R | S | E |

Vertical row: 1/2 2/4 4/4 4/- -/3 3/3 3/1 1/1
Horizontal row: 3/4 4/1 1/- -/- -/2 2/2 2/3

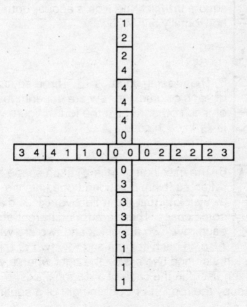

| 1 | 2 | 3 | 5 |
|---|---|---|---|
| 4 | 3 | 7 | 10 |
| 5 | 5 | 10 | 15 |
| 9 | 8 | 17 | 25 |

1. The missing number is 10. Along each row and down each column, pairs of numbers add up to give the next number – e.g., in the top row 1+2 = 3, 2 + 3 = 5.

2. The missing figure is ⊡. In each row and column the circle occupies four different positions – top, bottom, left and right.

| 14 | 10 | 12 | 12 |
|----|----|----|----|
| 7 | 17 | 1 | 23 |
| 20 | 4 | 15 | 9 |
| 16 | 8 | 5 | 19 |

3. The missing number is 1. The grid is vertically divided in half. Each half along every row adds up to 24 – e.g., 14 + 10, 7 + 17, 20 + 4, etc.

| T | A | L | E |
|---|---|---|---|
| A | X | I | S |
| L | I | M | P |
| E | S | P | Y |

4. The missing letter is E. This is a magic word square in which the words appear both horizontally and vertically.

5. The missing figure is ◩. Three squares of each column and row are superimposed on each other to give the fourth figure which is ⧆ in each case.

6. The missing figure is ⬚ Each shape has a reflected 'twin' positioned one knight's move away. Note that the reflective axis is diagonal in some cases. There are four different shapes in each row. Two are black and two are white.
    Also, in each column and row two of the shapes are on the left side and two are on the right when a vertical axis has been used. In the case of a diagonal axis, the shapes occupy the top left or bottom right of a square.

Rating: 2 fair; 3 good; 4 very good; 5 excellent; 6 exceptional

Poison: substitute each 'times' with the letter X.

There are 100 different creatures, more if you count 'pen' in paragraph one and 'cur' in paragraph three

A DRAMATIC ESCAPE

I had spent the night in gale-force winds, forced to share a foxhole with a cocky, poxy fellow who would ask unkindly 'Want your mother, then?', and a nameless, naked man. A teeming downpour made us so wet and my kit ten times heavier as I perched on a board, sipping water from a ewer and a pan the rain filled.

Now it was hot, terribly hot – and eerily quiet. Suddenly the crude music of the bugle was playing 'Up and at 'em!' We charged sluggishly, puffing hard in the heat, unable to breathe. Bullets were flying, but I was unscathed as I ducked and weaved to and fro, grasping my lucky amulet. I chose my path awkwardly but shrewdly, based on key points of army doctrine.

A gleam caught my eye, a rifle aimed at me. Then a bang. I dove into a hole, landing heavily. The round bounced off my helmet, nicked my thumb and bowled the Lieutenant over. He became I imp, a last agonized groan and stench marked his final breath. 'O God, O God!' I cursed, feeling sadder and more anti-war than ever. Why did I sign up for a combat command? It was a bleeding horror, a nightmare. I'd rather be a raw rookie in the sixth (or seventh) battalion, not a hero – a chaplain rather.

That made me pause a little and think of the Gospel. 'I cannot abide more vile murder. I'll go AWOL for a while,' I decided. It was now or, maybe, never. So I fled with the man I liked the most, Richards (Bill), a coy, pure chap, who had also been badly shaken by the carnage. We weren't craven cowards, or cared a cent who thought so. But neither of us wanted to endure what could be a very long war.

We crept through a tunnel, keeping low, to a road. I followed the map I kept in my pigskin pouch. I wished for the car I bought a month ago, a Triumph with new tyres and the famous emblem. No car passed by, so we had to hijack a lorry, then took steerage berths on a boat heading overseas. And so we both rushed to freedom. I had a bout of catarrh, in other respects I'm now hale and far healthier, and my thumb is on the mend. We now rent a cottage away from all the danger, Bill and I, and live in peace studying molecular biology and playing Scrabble.

1. A park of guns; 2. A brew of beer; 3. A drove of kine; 4. A yoke of oxen; 5. A leash of bucks; 6. A knob of toads; 7. A thicket of trees; 8. A skein of geese; 9. A cast of hawks; 10. A community of saints; 11. A covey of grouse; 12. A team of horses; 13. A bunch of widgeon; 14. A flight of dunlin; 15. A muster of peacocks; 16. A lepe of leopards; 17. A sedge of bitterns; 18. A herd of giraffes; 19. A troop of kangaroos

| K | | L | B | U | N | C | H | D |
|---|---|---|---|---|---|---|---|---|
| N | | E | M | U | S | T | E | R |
| O | T | P | A | R | K | | R | O |
| B | R | E | W | | E | F | D | V |
| C | O | V | E | Y | I | L | | E |
| C | O | M | M | U | N | I | T | Y |
| A | P | | S | E | D | G | E | O |
| S | | L | E | A | S | H | A | K |
| T | H | I | C | K | E | T | M | E |

48: transpose the digits of the last number and subtract the previous one: $51 - 24 = 27$; $75 - 27 = 48$.

W: it is the only one of the letters that can also be added to 'it' to form a word.

2:1 in favour of John: $((20/30)^2)*100$ compared with $((20/60)^2)*200$

| | 1 | 2 | 3 | 4 |
|---|---|---|---|---|
| 1 | DIS | PAR | AGE | D |
| 2 | C | A | N | AL |
| 3 | U | D | D | ER |
| 4 | S | IGM | A | S |

# IQ TESTS

This test consists of a battery of 30 questions designed to test your powers of vocabulary, calculation and logical reasoning. There is a time limit of 60 minutes for completing the test in one sitting. You should keep strictly to the time limit because your score will be invalidated if it is exceeded, so work as quickly as you can.

The answers are on page 126.

**1.** Which is the odd one out?

chronical, record, diary, account, book, journal

**2.** Bill and Ben share flower pots in the ratio of 3:5. If Ben has 300 flower pots, how many has Bill?

A. 54    B. 100    C. 120    D. 180    E. 240

**3.** Which two of the following words have opposite meanings?

slimness, glut, mucilage, banter, paucity, veneer

**4.** What two letters continue the following sequence?

ND, ND, ESD, NES, RS

**5.** Dilemma is to quandary as flight is to

A. danger   B. predicament   C. puzzle
D. confound   E. bewilderment

**6.** If the score on 12 dice totals 36, what is the average of the scores on the opposite side?

A. 2   B. 3   C. 4   D. 5   E.6

**7.** What word belongs in the brackets?

FINESSE (SNAIL) FACILE
FELSPAR ( . . . . . ) ATTIRE

**8.** Sid, Alf and Jim wish to share out a certain sum of money between them. Sid gets ²/₅, Alf gets 0.45 and Jim gets £210. How much is the original amount of money?

A. £800   B. £1000   C. £1200
D. £1400   E. £1600

**9.** Which two of the following words are closest in meaning?

sanguine, anaemic, opulent, worried, pallid, dissolute

**10.** What is the next number in this sequence?

1, 2, 3, 7, 22

**11.** Alf is half again as old as Jim, who is half again as old as Sid. Their ages total 133. How old is Jim?

A. 30   B. 35   C. 36   D. 40   E. 42   F. 48

**12.** Which of the words in brackets is opposite in meaning to the word in capitals?

TRIVIAL
(large, packed, significant, radiant, blatant)

**13.** Which is the odd one out?

nutmeg, beige, mocha, sable, umber

**14.** Agri- is to soil as omni- is to

A. full   B. all   C. large   D. ever   E. single

**15.** In greyhound racing, a favourite bet in a field of six runners is to try to forecast the first two dogs in the correct order. In a field of six runners, how many different ways are there in which the first two places can be filled.

A. 20   B. 30   C. 120   D. 240   E. 720

**16.** What word means the same as the definitions outside the brackets?

benevolent ( . . . . ) genus

**17.** Which of the words in brackets has the same meaning as the word in capitals?

RIPOSTE (blow, retort, fence, gamble, argue)

**18.** Horology is to time as dendrology is to

A. hair   B. plants   C. trees   D. teeth   E. soil

**19.** If six apples and six oranges cost 60p and seven apples and one orange cost 52p how much does one apple cost?

**20.** Which two of the following words have opposite meanings?

original, natural, groundless, basic, proven, infinite

**21.** Which is the odd one out?

calm, quiet, relaxed, serene, unruffled

**22.** Imagine two bags. Each bag contains six balls: two red, two yellow and two black. One ball is drawn out of each bag. What are the chances that at least one of the balls will be black?

A. 1 in 3   B. 2 in 3   C. 3 in 4
D. 5 in 6   E. 5 in 9   F. 7 in 9

**23.** What word means the same as the definitions outside the brackets?

fictional work ( . . . . . ) original

**24.** Firm is to flabby as piquant is to

A. small   B. pleasant   C. large
D. salty   E. bland

**25.** Which of the words in the brackets has the same meaning as the word in capitals?

CORROBORATION (enunciation, litigation, censure, proof, interaction)

**26.** Sid's house is seventh from one end of the row and eleventh from the other end. How many houses are there in the row?

A. 15   B. 16   C. 17   D. 18   E. 19   F. 20

**27.** Pittance is to peanuts as platitudinous is to

A. walnuts   B. stroppy   C. disk
D. corny   E. wishy-washy

**28.** Which is the odd one out?

marshal, surround, activate, mobilize, rally

**29.** Which two of the following words are closest in meaning?

convert, device, transform, communicate, displace, condemn

**30.** Which two of the following words have the opposite meanings?

gregarious, frugal, antisocial, abstemious, lonely, adaptable

This is a culture-fair test, designed to test your powers of logical reasoning and your understanding of relationships, pattern and design. Study each display of diagrams and select the one option from each choice given. Study the instructions to each question. You have a time limit of 20 minutes to complete the 10 questions in one sitting. You should keep strictly to the time limit, as your score will be invalidated if this is exceeded, so work as quickly as possible.

The answers are on page 126.

**1.** Which option – A, B, C, D or E – continues the sequence?

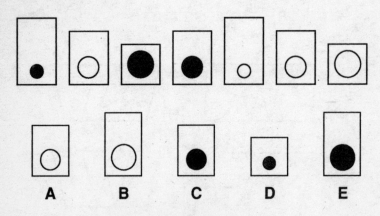

**2.** Which is the odd one out?

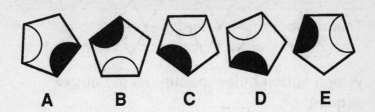

A  B  C  D  E

**3.**

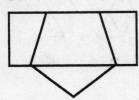 is to 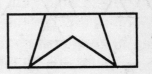 as

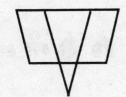 is to

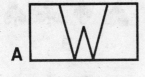  

A  B

C  D

**4.**

## Which option below continues the above sequence?

**A**      **B**      **C**      **D**      **E**

**5.**

  is to  as

 is to

**A**

**B**

**C**              **D**

**6.**

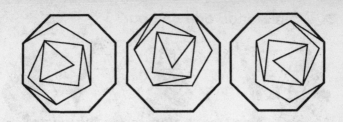

Which option below continues the above
sequence?

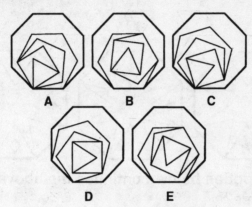

**7.**

Which option continues the above sequence?

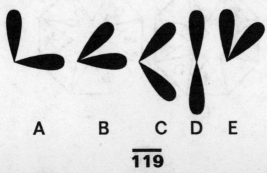

A    B    C    D    E

**8.** Which is the odd one out?

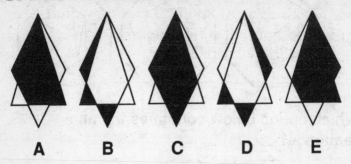

A    B    C    D    E

**9.**

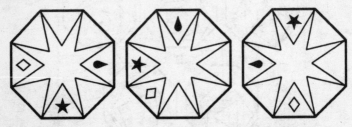

Which option below continues the above sequence?

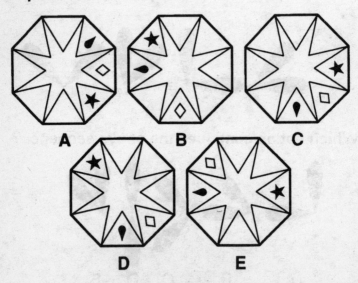

A    B    C

D    E

**10.** Look along each horizontal line and down each vertical line and decide which of the options following belongs in the empty square.

A     B     C     D     E

In this test you are to circle from the four words on the right the one you think has the closest association with the word in capitals. The word will not necessarily mean the same as or even the opposite of the key word but will relate to it. Give yourself any reasonable time to complete the test. Do not use aids to memory. What we are here trying to gauge is your feel for words. The test should be completed in one single setting.

The answers are on page 127.

1. ACRIMONY
   abuse taxation accounting chess
2. ACUMEN
   brain thought judgement examination
3. TRANSVERT     level smooth revert turn
4. MAYHEM        sex offend injure soften
5. BRUSQUE
   curt sensitive confident egotistic
6. VILIFY        slight sight right might
7. POIGNANT   sickness illness grief animal
8. GREGARIAN       alone one mob scenery
9. SORORICIDE
   sisterhood brotherhood womanhood death
10. SOCIOGENY
    science fight society picture

11. TREPIDATION
          betterment torpedo tremble trick
12. HALLOW          tighten simplify levy raise
13. ERGONOMICS          place work fish time
14. SPIFFLICATE          lecture run claim crush
15. ARROGATE   arrogant think usurp plunder
16. SPUMESCENT   whales wales wails foam
17. KLAXON          sound angel ribbon wind
18. RETICULE          fence grid gate cog
19. CONCIERGE
          wife child mother manageress
20. BROUHAHA          hubbub job dance fire
21. PROVOST          lead sun drink drunk
22. COMBE          tree comb hair valley
23. MAMMOPLASTY bed tank foot restoration
24. PSYCHEDELIC
          drug mind addiction ancient
25. PALAEONTOLOGY
          leg intestine throat bones
26. ABNEGATE          abjure size paint level
27. ANADONIA
          strength speed feeling cleverness
28. DEHORTATION
          rhyme rhythm speech redness
29. POLLICITATION
          seek policeman find promise
30. ENNUI
     jobber weakness weariness disinterest
31. PHENGITE          kerchief beard boot metal
32. ANOESIS
          consciousness game song garden

33. MERKIN          wig club door eye
34. ANODYNAL
          tallness harmless sickness feeling
35. TELENOMY
          telescope tallow purpose telegraph
36. STILLAGE          owl cup frame orange
37. COMPLANATE     boss hang level smooth
38. RUNIC          foreign up down single
39. CONCYCLIC
          circumference point edge epicycle
40. ECBOLIC
  parturition slavery economics econometrics
41. REMONSTRATE
          expostulate charge simplify score
42. DISCULPATE     knob insult gain blame
43. BUCCINAL  hornish bookish blackish silly
44. DEREQUISITION
          crime cities property starvation
45. MYSOPHOBIA          dirt shift shirt left
46. PANDICULATION  trace callow stretch lift
47. MYOSIS
          contraction binding change sleep
48. MORIOPLASTY  loss sighting pitch sharing
49. PRAETOR          science book head tail
50. INFIBULATION       hair clasp dart head
51. RICTUS          crater moon grin grind
52. EMICTION
          urination watering salting eating
53. KWASHIORKOR     track steal sink food
54. ALNASCHARISM
          dreams habit living friendship

55. ZETETIC        zodiac sleep time enquiry

56. FOLIA       ift turnbuckle music linoleum

57. GIPPO        soup scoop troop hoop

58. TABULA-RASA

       experience effort space wilderness

59. TRIDE   speed hardness sickly astronomer

60. FIBONACCI

      order priesthood sainthood church

61. FULGID      full bright childhood flow

62. RECIDIVIST

      charity crime hospitals income

63. DYSRHYTHMIA    tail insects pilot bate

64. MACERATE   fat lean heighten encourage

65. PLEBICOLIST

      courtship fighter stranger maid

66. ONEIROLOGY

     interpretation linguist words littoral

67. BURD       bird female gate diction

68. PTERYGIA     toe finger skin nail

69. ANTITHEMATIC

   standard forest systematization longing

70. ANTISTASIS

     reverse hand sorrow hangover

## Test 1

**1.** book, **2.** 180, **3.** glut/paucity, **4.** ID (they are the middle letters extracted from the days of the week, starting with suNDday),
**5.** predicament, **6.** 4 (opposite sides of a die always total 7), 7. alter (code $FI_4N_2ESS_1E$ – SNAIL – $FA_3CIL_5E$; use corresponding letters in the second set of words), **8.** £1400,
**9.** anaemic/pallid, **10.** 155 ($1\times2+1=3$, $2\times3+1=7$, $3\times7+1=22$, $7\times22+1=155$), **11.** 42,
**12.** significant, **13.** sable, **14.** all, **15.** 30 ($=6\times5$), **16.** kind, **17.** retort, **18.** trees,
**19.** 7p, **20.** groundless/proven, **21.** quiet,
**22.** 5 in 9, **23.** novel, **24.** bland, **25.** proof,
**26.** 17, **27.** corny, **28.** surround, **29.** convert/transform, **30.** gregarious/antisocial.

| | |
|---|---|
| 12-15 | Average |
| 16-21 | Good |
| 22-27 | Very good |
| 28-30 | Exceptional |

## Test 2

**1.** C; **2.** B; **3.** D; **4.** A; **5.** B; **6.** B; **7.** E;
**8.** C; **9.** C; **10.** D

| | |
|---|---|
| 4-5 | Average |
| 6-7 | Good |
| 8-9 | Very good |
| 10 | Exceptional |

*Note*: Tests 1 and 2 have been specifically compiled for this book, so an actual IQ rating cannot be given.

# Test 3

1. abuse, **2.** judgement, **3.** turn, **4.** injure,
**5.** curt, **6.** slight, **7.** grief, **8.** mob, **9.** death,
**10.** society, **11.** tremble, **12.** raise,
**13.** work, **14.** crush, **15.** usurp, **16.** foam,
**17.** sound, **18.** grid, **19.** manageress,
**20.** hubbub, **21.** lead, **22.** valley,
**23.** restoration, **24.** mind, **25.** bones,
**26.** abjure, **27.** feeling, **28.** speech,
**29.** promise, **30.** weariness, **31.** metal,
**32.** consciousness, **33.** wig, **34.** harmless,
**35.** purpose, **36.** frame, **37.** level,
**38.** foreign, **39.** circumference,
**40.** parturition, **41.** expostulate, **42.** blame,
**43.** hornish, **44.** property, **45.** dirt,
**46.** stretch, **47.** contraction, **48.** loss,
**49.** head. **50.** clasp. **51.** grin,
**52.** urination, **53.** food, **54.** dreams,
**55.** enquiry, **56.** music, **57.** soup,
**58.** experience, **59.** speed, **60.** order,
**61.** bright, **62.** crime, **63.** pilot, **64.** lean,
**65.** courtship, **66.** interpretation,
**67.** female, **68.** skin, **69.** standard,
**70.** sorrow.

See page 128 for an assessment rating for test 3.

# The table is for the general adult population only

## Source: I.S.P.E. selection

| WITH | | | |
|---|---|---|---|
| *14 | – | Top | 55% |
| *15 | – | | 50 |
| *16 | – | | 45 |
| 17 | – | | 40 |
| 18 | – | | 35 |
| 19 | – | | 30 |
| 20 | – | | 25 |
| 21 | – | | 20 |
| 22 | – | | 15 |
| 23 | – | | 12 |
| 24 | – | | 10 |
| 25 | – | | 8 |
| 26 | – | | 7 |
| 27 | – | | 6 |
| 29 | – | | 5 |
| 30 | – | | 4 |
| 32 | – | | 3 |
| 35 | – | | 2 |
| 39 | – | | 1 |
| 40 | – | | 0.9 |
| 41 | – | | 0.8 |
| 42 | – | | 0.7 |
| 43 | – | | 0.6 |
| 44 | – | | 0.5 |
| 45 | – | | 0.4 |
| 46 | – | | 0.3 |
| 48 | – | | 0.2 |
| 52 | – | | 0.1 |
| 53 | – | | 0.08 |
| 54 | – | | 0.07 |
| 55 | – | | 0.05 |
| 56 | – | | 0.03 |
| 58 | – | | 0.02 |
| 60 | – | | 0.01 |
| 61 | – | | 0.006 |
| 62 | – | | 0.004 |
| 63 | – | | 0.002 |

Highest known score = 65 Top 0.0004%; 70 = test ceiling

* average